Introduction

We live in amazing times.

While much of the world may seem chaotic and scary, it really is a time of great opportunity. Opportunity and dare I say a time of revolution in both western society and business as a result of digital technologies.

Is there anything you or I cannot create today?

Look around and the answer seems to be 'no.' There are very few business problems we cannot tackle. There are almost no technological barriers today, thanks to digital software and hardware advances. We see entrepreneurs achieving feats once reserved only for science fiction.

This new age has unfolded before our eyes, with significant advances in just the last five or ten years. The only limitation might be our imagination.

Do you want to go into outer space? Elon Musk, Richard Branson, Peter Diamandis and Jeff Bezos seem to think it's not only possible, but they're making it probable in short order. Soon everyday men and women will be able to travel into space. Companies may be able to explore and leverage untold assets in our galaxy within the next decade.

Want to build electric cars? Tesla, Fisker and even big automakers like Toyota, Ford, GM and BMW have sold over two million electric cars around the world since 2008. Just a decade ago, the concept of an electric car on American roads seemed like a fantasy.

Do you want to develop a business around an Artificial Intelligence (AI)? Amazon, Google and Apple all offer AI that orders groceries; plays our favorite music; turns the lights at home on or off upon command; controls the temperature on the thermostat; or finds the answer to our most pressing questions. Apple's Siri, Amazon's Alexa, Google's Assistant and even the Open AI project from Elon Musk all offer developers and consumers platforms that can be used today as an AI-based digital personal assistant.

Want to build a business where drones carry your packages to customers? The nascent drone market is both a current reality and an opportunity for many future uses. FedEx, Amazon and UPS are all testing home delivery drones. An entire ecosystem is springing up around this technology.

What about creating goods out of thin air with a Star Trek-like replicator? The rise of 3-D printing technology is allowing on-the-spot creation of everything from prosthetic arms to weapons to blood vessels and beyond.

How about being able to create simple software applications from the spark of an idea? With little more than an idea you can begin a project to create mobile apps for iPhone and Android. Within months of thinking about an idea for an app, normally average people have been inspired to create mobile apps and to launch them on iTunes or Google Play stores. Less than nine years ago, this concept didn't even exist.

These are just some of the examples of how digital technology has created both application development or product ecosystems that empower entrepreneurs and consumers alike. These ecosystems allow creative business people to dramatically impact product categories and industries. A new future is unfolding before our eyes with winners and losers being chosen daily.

As an Entrepreneur your number one task right now should be applying ideas that either automate or grow your business using digital technology.

Automate and Grow is an approach to harnessing the possibilities of digital technology for your business. Embracing this concept will take a plan and some effort. Entrepreneurs and business leaders today have the opportunity to understand and embrace this approach that promises the freedom to develop amazing new products, services and approaches to automating marketing, sales and customer support.

Digital Revolution

The industrial revolution was all about leverage.

Getting more production by using systems, tools and machines that sped up and automated processes on a mass scale. This was particularly true around the textile and agricultural industries.

The digital revolution by contrast has been about the proliferation of data and information and now also web and mobile based software applications. Creating markets and value around apps and information. This digital era started during the 1980s and is ongoing. The **Digital Revolution** is sometimes also called the Third Industrial **Revolution**. The next phase of the digital revolution is about automating digital tech, making it autonomous.

If you're reading this, maybe you are thinking about starting a business or maybe you are a leader in a business. Are

13

you frustrated by the pain of manual processes in your business? Perhaps your business doesn't collect and utilize the information on prospects and customers that it needs to. You may collect customer information but don't have systems in place to manage that data.

Maybe you've identified a way to use apps, software or other digital assets like websites and web apps to address an untapped market need.

Are you even attempting to leverage digital technology?Are you effectively using Software as a Service (SaaS), websites, mobile applications or other digital tools in key areas of your business?

If your company doesn't have a digital strategy, then look at your competition. If they are using digital technology to improve customer experience or to improve business operations, then you are at a serious disadvantage.

If you are looking for help to map out a plan and to implement digital innovation; to automate and grow your business, then this is the book for you.

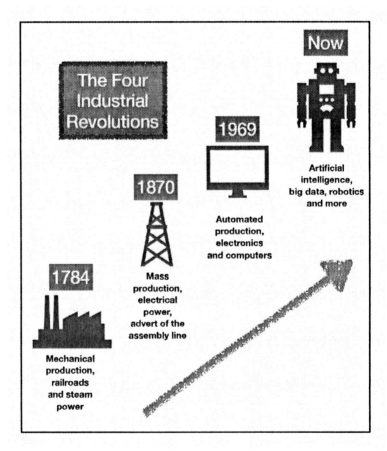

Source: Twitter Post by physician-scientist, author, editor Eric Topal.

If you're reading this, maybe you're either thinking about starting a business, currently operate or lead a business. Maybe you're sick of the pain of manual processes. Perhaps your business doesn't collect and utilize the information on prospects and customers that it needs to. You may collect it but don't have systems in place to manage that data. Maybe you've identified a way to use apps, software, robots or your website to address an untapped market need.

The question is, are you even attempting to leverage digital automation? It is important to ask yourself: is your business effectively using Software as a Service, websites, mobile applications and other digital tools in key business areas.

If you don't have your own digital strategy, then look at your competition. If they are effectively using digital technology to improve customer experience or to improve business operations, then you are at a serious disadvantage.

If you are looking for help to map out a plan and to implement digital innovation, automation and growth in your business then this is the book for you.

If you are an entrepreneur the best way to improve your business life is by implementing some sort of digital strategy. The mandate of that digital strategy is to Automate and Grow your business. If you want to strategically make your business run better, attract more customers and keep those customers, then read on.

Uber Effect

Perhaps the greatest current day example of a company who leveraged the power of digital automation to achieve growth is Uber. In case you're not aware of Uber (hey, it's possible), it's a ride-sharing, ride-hailing app business that has disrupted the taxi business all around the world.

While they have had some media controversies along the way, there is little denying they've expanded the business of driving people around, perhaps beyond even the original addressable market of passengers that were being serviced by alternatives.

They're a great example of a company who automated both customer & employee-facing processes to solve problems. They generated both supply and demand using mobile apps, marketing automation and Software as a Service. It's hard to dispute they use all of these to improve the customer experience of their ideal client.

Uber, as a result, grew not just their business, but actually an entire category of service. They created a technological advantage so great that they were almost a monopoly. Now, a ride-sharing competitor, Lyft however, has emerged in an almost parallel fashion so that they are not the only market entrant. Together, however, they have lapped the traditional taxi businesses.

Source: Forbes: Impact of Uber on the Taxi Industry

Uber did this by, amongst other things, using an app and a back-end software platform to organize and monetize the cars used by limo drivers and then individuals, who were never drivers of passengers before. They unlocked two unused resources, the time of non-professional drivers and their cars, to move what were traditional taxi customers but also non-traditional passengers around.

Furthermore, Uber has killed the taxi business by driving the cost of getting transported around, while increasing the convenience for potential passengers, those who previously would never have taken a taxi. So, they changed the demand curve.

Incumbent Taxi Business Response

Taxi companies are trying to respond to a universal change that has become a verb. *'Let's Uber.'* They've vainly tried to legislate and guilt people into supporting a lesser product. (That didn't work). In some cities, taxi companies have tried to use a mobile app to dispatch drivers across multiple cab companies or individual cab companies. In the end, though, this is a three-horse race. Uber, it's actual competitor, Lyft and the old school taxi business.

You can take away the pains of the consumer, address the challenges of operating a business by hopscotching over old entrenched methods and technology to operate a new business that targets the same customers. If it's excellent enough you can attract new customers. That is of course the point of this whole idea of Automate + Grow.

Decide Which Business You Want

Answer this now: Which business would you rather work for, lead or own? The one that is shrinking and struggling under the tide of technology, new consumer expectations for speed, quality, communication and even payment or the business operating within a new paradigm? The business that is automated and operating in an efficient manner buoyed by digital trends and technology that will crush competitors who do not have an Automate + Grow strategy?

How to Automate and Grow

There are a couple of steps to get to the point where you're on the right demand curve. You start at the beginning so we have a nice foundation to build upon. All cards on the table.

- The first will be to evaluate your market.
- The second is to evaluate your competitors.
- The third is to evaluate your business.

Then imagine something that changes the game. Think of how specifically the application of a digital technology would create a new demand curve. How a problem your customers face could be solved by that digital technology and how applying both customer facing and internal digital automation will shift customer demand to your paradigm.

Perhaps it is a product or service delivery enhancement. Maybe it is a new level of operational excellence that makes your business stand out. By thinking in these terms you can begin to imagine new digital and non-digital advantages you will hold over competitors.

Figure Out the Gap

What resources do you need to move your business into that new demand curve? Once you have these basics, you can begin to address your key business functions one by one to gain leverage.

The point of Automate + Grow is to give you as a start-up, small or medium sized business, a framework to not just survive but thrive in a marketplace of new ideas and so-called disruptors.

Why Automate?

This is not just a matter of 'do it because everyone else is doing it.' On the contrary, Uber is not successful simply because they automated a process of hailing a cab. They created an entire system to eliminate constraints in the process of getting a vehicle to a passenger, getting that passenger from A to B.

They made a system not stuck in the previous system. So really what they did was innovate. Their innovation was realized when they built an entire software and application platform to streamline what was a very disjointed and manual process with cabs.

Life Before Uber

Try to recall, if you can, the days when there was no Uber and the process of getting a ride in a cab was painful and expensive.

Step 1: Hail a cab. Hope there is one driving by you that isn't occupied. Does anyone know the formula here? When the lights are on does that mean it's taken? Does it mean it's available? Not sure about you, but I could never figure this out in the rare circumstance where I would subject myself to the pain of taking a taxi, which in the past was rare.

Option 1b: Call a taxi cab company, but which company? What is the number? Searching.... searching... there are a few. Search the internet, call them, have a difficult analog conversation to explain who you are, where you are, hope you can get a cab to pick you up. Yay. So not fun.

Uber Automated Innovation: You open an iPhone or Android app. You confirm your location. You push a button. A driver is en route. You never have to speak to anyone and play the broken telephone game.

Step 2: Wait for a cab.

Ok, you've called a taxi cab company. Great! Now you hope that your cab shows up and that the dispatch who is using a 2-way radio (an old school walkie talkie) to bark out jobs to the taxis in the most analog way imaginable—by voice to a group over a loudspeaker in their cars. Some may have invested in automated digital dispatch actually. Those did exist, for sure. In either case, the dispatcher routes a driver towards you and in the process of collecting your information, they try to roughly communicate when they'll show up, if they do.

Dispatch in crackly, stressed-out nicotine and coffee-fueled voice: "What is your ETA Cabby #3468, over?"
Driver: "Dispatch, I guess I'll be there in 22 minutes."

Of course, the driver has no idea what you look like and has to hunt and peck to find you when he shows up.

Uber Automated Innovation: You see on the app using GPS and unicorn magic, how much time it will be until your driver arrives. You can even watch their little car on a map as it gets closer. You see picture of the driver, his car, and his license plate number. He sees on the app a profile of you: your name, your picture. Thus, everyone finds each other without much hassle or stress.

P.S. Any idea which taxi doesn't suck? Oh yeah, that leads to step #3 in taxi cabbing.

21

Step 3: Get in the cab. Hope it doesn't smell, isn't dirty and hope that you can give your address to the driver and get somewhere.

What if it does suck? Well you can always call the cab company back and complain. What does that accomplish? Not sure. There isn't a measurable way to provide feedback on the driver.

Uber Automated Innovation: Driver Ratings! You can see the rating of your driver by previous passengers. You can rate your driver. Be warned, they can rate you too, so be nice. Oh, and then because there are ratings (out of 5) Uber can get rid of the bad drivers. Heck, they can measure and enforce standards of cleanliness, driving, courtesy, etc. Take that, cab company!

Step 4: Drive to your destination in the cab. "Hey, what route are you taking, Mr. Cab Driver?" Also...Is he a maniac? When will we get there?

Uber Automation Innovation: GPS routing. You can see the route because the driver is given a route. It's not a mystery. Everything is in front of you.

Think about Step #5: Pay for your taxi cab ride.

OK, there is a meter, without any rhyme or reason (well, nothing you can anticipate) to determine the cost of your ride. Is it based upon distance? Is it based upon time in the cab?

Sure, yes, both, neither. Who knows, you just sit there and watch as the meter tick, tick, ticks up.

When you arrive, the meter finally stops. For riders watching the cost of their ride on the meter as they travel can be a source of stress. Watching as money flies out of their pocket before their very eyes. Not exactly a great customer experience.

Uber Automation Innovation: Fixed fares before you book. Uber uses your location, your destination, the traffic, and the volume of demand to pre-set the ride cost. People complain about "flex" pricing. Wait, what do you think happens when a cabbie gets stuck in traffic? Oh yeah, the meter keeps on ticking up, up, up. Still, better to know ahead of time.

Step 6: Pay for the cab.

You: "Do you take credit cards?"
Taxi: "GRRR you pay cash? Pay Cash. You leave tip?"

Ok so that's a nightmare.

Uber Automation Innovation: The fare was pre-set. Up until recently, the tip was included. No haggling over currency, change, hoping they take credit cards. It's simple you hop in, you hop out, it's paid for automagically.

Is Your Business Your Nightmare or Your Dream?

There are a few ugly steps above that would make operating a cab company, as well as contracting a cab company, total chaos and a purely hateful experience, wouldn't you say?

Is this your business?

Are you a bunch of crazy humans running around making up rules and processes like plugging holes on a dam?

Are you preventing efficient and effective allocation of your company's resources, massive buying by customers and massive organization of service or product delivery because you refuse to automate? Maybe you've never thought along these lines, but technology to automate has really a twofold potential payoff.

- Makes it easier for you to deliver your product or service
- Makes it easier for your customer to find, consume and pay for your product or service

The Emotional Barriers to Automation

There are four common roadblocks that prevent you from investing in software, apps or other tools that would automate your business.

- Time
- Money
- Knowledge
- Guilt

We will address the overall apprehension in chapters 1 and 2, but to summarize quickly consider:

Time. How long is it going to take me to find, define, buy and/or build a software system or app? This is going to take years! I don't have the time to make this happen.

Money. How much is this going to cost me? I could never afford to pull this off. You likely cannot afford NOT to do this, but we will cross this bridge later.

Knowledge. What do I buy? What do I build? How do I build it? What technology? Do I need to hire developers from India so it's cheap?

In determining your automation plan, this book will outline how you figure all this out. It will help you overcome these barriers and to get beyond the fear, uncertainty and doubt that goes along with the above three roadblocks to Automation Nirvana.

Indeed, Automate and Grow is as much a mantra as it is a guide to getting this done.

Guilt

'If I automate that "x process" then, that's Betty's job. Aren't we killing Betty's job?

Maybe, but have you ever wondered if Betty would rather be doing something other than shuffling papers, making up processes, fixing messes—the same messes over and over? Compiling spreadsheets, telling customers, 'Sorry, this is how we do it. That's how the crazy owner wants to do it because of ABC.'

If you automate, you're likely freeing up someone's time from something horribly repetitive, broken and inefficient. Now you can put that person to better use, make their job easier, more fun even.

To overcome the guilt of automation (you know some of you have this in your brain), you need to think ahead now. How do I make happier people do more important and fulfilling things for the money I'm spending on their time and mind?

Ask them! We'll get to that as we talk about GROWTH, because people in your business should be part of the growth and innovation plan as much as they are about the automation plan.

You goal is simple, if not altruistic. Free people from the mundane, the silly and the downright stupid tasks that chew up their time and attention. Set them free to do more creative, high value things that are more fulfilling.

Lofty, yes, but this innovative thinking needs to be at the heart of our mantra of Automate + Grow.

You Need a Strategy

Alright so I can bombard you with case study after case study of how companies have disrupted an industry, innovated and created a new demand curve for customers using automate + grow strategies.

AirBNB, GrubHub, Plated/Blue Apron...uh Amazon?.. Ya Amazon, lets not forget that little business.

Let's assume you are convinced. Great, now what? You need to create a written strategy.

- What does the market look like now?
- What is your vision for your market?
- What problem exists in the market?
- Who is your ideal customer?
- What is your mission?

- How can the problem be fixed and the mission fulfilled by applying a digital technology?

Creating a Strategic Plan

Once you have defined your Strategy you need an Automate and Grow plan. The plan will address in practical terms, how to apply the tactic of digital automation and it will have a plan for growth.

1. What systems or processes exist?
2. What new processes or systems are needed?
3. What data matters?
4. What reports exist now either in software or spreadsheets?
5. How do these processes, systems, applications and/or reports need to change?
6. What people resources exist?
7. How will people resources be freed from the pain of the mundane? How can you refocus people on high value work or replace their role?
8. What options are there for getting new digital tools like software as a service, websites or mobile apps? Will you buy, build or rent?

Your plan can and should address internal processes, customer-facing processes and, really, any function needed in the business..

This book is organized in chapters, but it is likely you will skip ahead to sections that appeal to the current situation you need to address.

The key sections center around the automation of three key customer-facing functions in your business that will impact growth:

- Marketing Automation
- Sales Automation
- Customer Service or Support Automation

Along the way, I try to provide three things in each chapter:

1. A framework for you to create a written plan around each of these functions;
2. Insight into capabilities you want to build that either approach technology or that people can address;
3. Examples, Insights or Ideas from other sources of material that I think are beneficial for you to review.

In the end, this Automate and Grow approach can be a one-time way for you to boost your business out of the dark ages. It can also become a part of your company culture where you continually seek ways to automate customer-facing or internal processes while you continue to add new prospects, clients, as well as new products, services or software that they want.

Why Write Automate and Grow?

In 2010, I was on my way out of a corporate job into the wild wilderness. With a package in hand, I had time and money to decide what I was going to do.

I decided that I was going to put my knowledge of the mobile space to build a small agency building iPhone and Android applications for customers. The first person to reach out to me said he had an idea he thought I would be perfect to lead. I signed on and in the process of putting together a team to develop iPhone and iPad applications, was introduced to a platform called Salesforce.com.

I was familiar with Salesforce.com as a web-based Customer Relationship Management application (CRM) but what I was being shown was more than this.

In particular, Force.com blew my mind. Here was a web-based platform that allowed you to build other business applications on top of the Salesforce.com SaaS. I think the implications were a little bit to digest.

What did this mean exactly? Don't you build software, license it, install it on a server or host it as a web-based platform?

Over the course of a few months, we developed an application that was Salesforce.com back end with iPad front end. We entered this application into the Salesforce 2010 AppQuest developer competition.

Shockingly, Portable Intelligence managed to place us top 5 in the competition. Although we never parlayed this into commercial success, it opened my eyes how you could use this platform to escape from a traditional software model. It made me realize that beyond CRM, you could theoretically automate different lines of business using a hosted platform.

No need to buy servers, no need to write a complete software stack. Instead, you could focus upon the business process, the data you were collecting to build an automation.

29

Since then, I've been lucky to work on some exciting projects that automated business processes for customers.

Salesforce itself has done a great job of creating other lines of business applications on its platform to address not just Sales, but Marketing, Customer Service and even H/R and AI now.

This is not a book about Salesforce, however. They are a leader in the space and I continue to enjoy working as a Salesforce consultant.

This is a book about how to understand a new model for business.

Whether you're a startup or existing business, there is a model for creating an Automate and Grow strategy to your business.

You can follow the same process that thousands of businesses have by looking at processes that humans just would be better not performing inside of a business.

Whether it's Salesforce.com, another Software as a Service CRM offering or a custom business application, you have the ability as a small or medium-sized business to use technology to create a shift, internally with how you operate, but also how you innovate in customer-facing products, sales, marketing and service delivery.

It's an exciting time and Automate and Grow can be your blueprint to create an amazing plan for your business. A plan you can start implementing tomorrow.

Is your business stuck? Is it serving you well as an entrepreneur, is it serving employees and executives? Is it serving customers in a unique and exciting way?

If not, then you can do a reboot. Regardless of the state of your business, regardless of your comfort level with new technology, you can do it.

Rather than being outflanked by a technology-savvy competitor, by using the ideas and process in Automate + Grow, you can remake your business or even your industry.

At the very least, you can free human resources from routine, mundane roles and you can instead put people into internal or customer-facing roles that unleash their potential and interests.

For you as a business leader, you can have more information and control over your business while working less.

That's crazy, right?

I have seen it, however. You can change the game using apps, SaaS and a good to great game plan.

If you have technology in place today that just doesn't serve you well, if it is clunky, difficult to operate, doesn't give you a model for rapid changes, if it's just plain old painful and expensive, there's an alternative now.

You can replace old stuff with new stuff that has less total cost of ownership. BTW, we're not doing these crazy TCO calculations to justify your investment.

Instead, I'm going to try to crack your mind open and give you the power to innovate, not just automate.

Automation is great, but then there is Growth.

Growth doesn't just come from automation, although it can be a byproduct. By using digital technology as an advantage, as a difference maker, you're putting your business on a path towards growth.

Ask yourself: 'Is it painful for customers to deal with you? Is your business fun to buy from?' If not, Automate + Grow is potentially a way to change that. To transform your business using digital technologies and methodologies that improve the customer experience of new and existing customers alike.

In the end, there is no greater satisfaction than seeing the transformation of your business as a result of this process.

My goal is simple: I want to help 1,000,000 businesses transform, automate and get on their path to growth.

This approach will allow entrepreneurs and business leaders to free themselves from limitations in their business to remake it.

For startups, they don't have to follow someone else's model. They can disrupt an industry while creating a business that gives them financial and personal freedom.

Day in day out they can provide customers with an exciting experience, and employees with more fulfillment in their work and more fun.

References:

https://www.forbes.com/sites/adigaskell/2017/01/26/study-explores-the-impact-of-uber-on-the-taxi-industry/#1dcdb57616b0

https://twitter.com/erictopol/status/701465779389083648

https://3dprintingindustry.com/news/12-things-we-can-3d-print-in-medicine-right-now-42867/

Chapter 1: Getting Your House in Order

Is your business difficult to run? Maybe your business runs well but things aren't advancing, you're not growing. The first thing to ask yourself as a leader in your business is, *why? What's the problem?*

Is it competition? Is it a change in options or alternatives? Is it simply that you're difficult to deal with vs options in the market. Perhaps you lack systems and applications to run your business in a consistent and automated fashion.

While a good amount of this book is about adopting technology, it is going to be very difficult to effectively build and implement technology if a few parts of your business are not buttoned down. That includes your product, people and processes.

Create a Clear Message

What business are you in? What problem do you solve and how do you deliver an effective or unique solution to the problem that customers have? If this is not clear and formalized you will have confusion in your business about the purpose of the company. Employees, partners and frankly customers will be asking about this.

Get Your Message Out

Maybe you have an awesome product or service. Perhaps it's very clear and obvious the value you bring. If so you will need a plan and a process to get the message to prospective customers.

If you have not yet invested in digital content or marketing this will become part of your plan.

Maybe you're trying to use old school methods to get the word out and these are less and less effective. You cannot even track a return on investment or response rate to your marketing efforts. If digital content and marketing is confusing or overwhelming to you, then this is your opportunity to deal with the reality and to become a content producing marketer.

Your Automate and Grow Strategy will include a Traffic and Conversion plan that ensures that you are effectively finding and converting prospects that match your ideal client profile using content, digital assets and conversion tactics.

Consistently convert prospects into customers

If you are struggling with turning leads and prospects into customers, this is where we need to test, prove and then create an effective Sales Process. Maybe you have a process that works but you need to formalize it. Or maybe you need to create an automated sales funnel so that you can scale. This is where we build a Sales Playbook and invest in Sales Process Automation.

Retain customers

Customer retention can be a black hole for many businesses. How much do you invest to keep customers? Is it working? If you have trouble retaining customers maybe the issue is your product or service. Maybe once you've sold them, you fail to keep selling them, you fail to invest in a proactive customer success effort.

Have a Clear Advantage

This goes back to messaging somewhat, but also how to deliver on the promise of your business' message. There's a few options to consider here:

    a.   Do you make it easy for customers to buy?

    b.   Do they have a clear reason to buy?

    c.   Do your processes, team and supporting applications make it easy for your team to operate day to day?

People Power

Are your employees the right ones? Do they have the right attitude, skills and motivation to drive your business forward? Our goal is to not only attract and keep the right people but also to make sure they are empowered to do the right things.

If you have the right people with the right attributes, skills and attitude, you will want to make sure they stay with you. Usually the best people are attracted to work for the best companies. Maybe not the biggest company, but businesses that have some clear message. Businesses with a clear advantage that are providing a positive customer experience. A business that also provides a positive employee experience.

Nobody wants to work for a bad company. A company with no vision, customers who are unhappy and who aren't loyal because that business doesn't provide a positive customer experience. Great companies are buoyed by slick systems, software and processes and a mandate to empower employees to deliver great work and ideas.

Fund the Business Properly

Not having enough cash to execute a new technology or business plan can be a problem. Attracting money can be in three forms:

        a.   Investment
        b.   Sell more
        c.   Be more profitable

Generally 'selling more' (b) solves a lot of problems. That is assuming you're selling profitably (c). Funding can come externally by raising money. Not always but often if you are not selling more stuff and in a profitable manner in an existing business- often 'a' won't happen.

That is not an absolute truth of course. If you have a way to transform or disrupt your business using a digital technology, you may find investment to help you do this based upon future potential. The reality is that for most businesses this is an unlikely option and often applies to a minority of companies funded by Venture Capital investment.

Someone Will Be Disrupting Your Industry

Very few industries lack competition. Today, that competitive environment is being bolstered by hard-charging, venture-backed businesses with a mantra to disrupt or die.

Startups, startup incubators and venture capital firms are actively on the hunt to use mobile apps, web apps and models of business that shift demand from your product or service to some new product or service.

37

So the Automate + Grow mantra is about making your current business more efficient through automation.

It's also about growing that business.

Impacts of Digital Technology

The Harvard Business Review points to two major phases of digital technology on a sector.

1. Disruption by New Incumbents- new digitally enabled business models that aggressively compete with legacy business models emerge and these crush the revenue and success of the legacy model as consumers move to them
2. Imitation by Incumbents- this is where competition increases on the new trend curve as legacy businesses adapt to the new digital reality and begin to innovate.

The cost of not innovating is heavy. It is estimated in "The Case for Offensive Strategies in Response to Digital Disruption." that over half of annual revenue growth and one third of earnings growth from incumbents is wiped out when they do not adapt quickly enough to the new digital reality.

Source: 6 Digital Strategies, and Why Some Work Better than Others, Harvard Business review July 31, 2017

Maybe You Have a Niche Already

You have customers. Creating an Automate and Grow Strategic Plan is your way to scale an already established and successful niche.

Perhaps the new innovation in your industry is to develop a business that simplifies and automates internal processes and customer-facing processes. Making your business easier to deal with than competitors.

You can bet that your customers are seeing these improvements from competitors. Their website is better, it's more useful. There is a customer portal. There is a way to buy via an e-commerce website. There is an app that helps customers do more business with your competitor. Maybe your competition does an amazing job of acquiring new customers using marketing automation. They could be selling more or faster because they effectively use e-commerce and CRM to profile and advance opportunities through automated sales funnels.

Product Innovation

You need to consider as you develop a strategic plan how to apply digital technology to your industry in the form of new digital products.

I had an amazing economics professor at the University of Waterloo named Larry Smith. Larry has a fantastic TED Talk that you might want to check out. Larry teaches a course on Entrepreneurship at University of Waterloo that may have stoked me to be more of the rebel that I am and run off and start companies.

One concept that I always remember from Larry was the concept of "shifting" the demand curve: making the entire industry fight it out for the same customer, but on a curve of your choosing.

Really, this boils down to creating a disruption in your market.

Here is the spectrum I see as you create your Automate and Grow business strategy:

Is your Business...

→ Currently selling to customers?

→ Decide: How effectively?

→ Adopting a new digital technology? To improve product or operations?

→ What automations will improve your business?

→ Does this give you a competitive advantage?

Here is what an Automate and Grow Strategy can help you achieve in a reasonably short amount of time.

1. Provide you with more information to make decisions
2. Free employees to do their best work - not busy work
3. Improve the speed you find new prospects through Marketing Automation
4. Improve the volume or speed you close new sales via Sales Automation
5. Support customers so they stick around and/or buy more - Customer Success
6. Create new products or services that shift demand from current industry products or services...

derive more revenue from same customers or give you a competitive advantage....Innovate and Disrupt.

Are You in an Industry That is Ready for Disruption?

I recently checked out a page on Y combinator's web site titled "Calls for Entrepreneurs." Y Combinator is an American seed accelerator, started in March 2005. In 2017 Forbes ranked YC one of two "Platinum Plus Tier U.S. Accelerators". Fast Company has called YC "the world's most powerful start-up incubator"

Consider the seven generic strategies that business might use to respond to digital disruption.

1. **The Block Strategy**. Using all means available to inhibit the disruptor. These means can include claiming patent or copyright infringement, erecting regulatory hurdles, and using other legal barriers.

2. **The Milk Strategy**. Extracting the most value possible from vulnerable businesses while preparing for the inevitable disruption.

3. **The Invest in Disruption Model**. Actively investing in the disruptive threat, including disruptive technologies, human capabilities, digitized processes, or perhaps acquiring companies with these attributes

4. **The Disrupt the Current Business Strategy**. Launching a new product or service that competes directly with the disruptor, and leveraging inherent strengths such as size, market knowledge, brand, access to capital, and relationships to build the new business.

5. **The Retreat into a Strategic Niche Strategy**. Focusing on a profitable niche segment of the core market where disruption is less likely to occur (e.g. travel agents focusing on corporate travel, and complex itineraries, book sellers and publishers focusing on academia niche).

6. **The Redefine the Core Strategy**. Building an entirely new business model, often in an adjacent industry where it is possible to leverage existing knowledge and capabilities (e.g. IBM to consulting, Fujifilm to cosmetics).

7. **The Exit Strategy**. Exiting the business entirely and returning capital to investors, ideally through a sale of the business while value still exists (e.g. Myspace selling itself to Newscorp).

So needless to say our focus will be upon responses similar to those in numbers three and four. Automate and Grow is about embracing digital trends or setting them. Both in terms of product offering, delivery and operations. Not fighting those trends.

Are You in Any of These Industries?

Y Combinator recognizes that there are opportunities to attack customers in these industries. To me that's an obvious alert if I am a business in any of these spaces that there's a better way to operate and a better way to interact with customers.

1. Energy
2. A.I.
3. Robotics
4. Biotech
5. Healthcare
6. Pharmaceuticals
7. Education

8. Human Augmentation
9. VR and AR
10. Transportation & Housing
11. One Million Jobs
12. Programming Tools
13. Hollywood 2.0
14. Diversity
15. Enterprise Software
16. Financial Services
17. Computer Security
18. Global Health
19. Underserved Communities
20. Food and Farming
21. Mass Media
22. Improving Democracy
23. Future of Work
24. News
25. Water

Once you have articulated your problem, you're on the path to creating an Automate and Grow Strategy. If your problem, however, is fear of change, you can create all the plans and strategies you want. Somewhere along the line you're going to self-sabotage those plans, coming up with reasons the investment of time, money and people won't be a good idea. It could be helpful to address the reasons you might be resisting change. Think about why you might be resisting implementing a technology plan to help your business thrive.

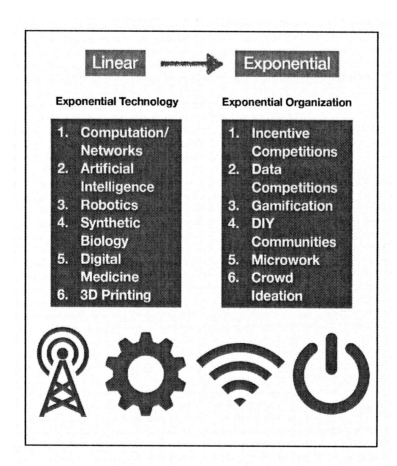

There are six exponential technologies that will transform industries. Can any of these be used to change your business?

Automate and Grow is primarily about how to apply number one on that list, computations and networks, to transform your business. Automate your business, primarily the marketing, sales and service functions using digital platforms.

At the same time lets be clear that offering new digital products or services to customers is also an effective way to grow. In some cases it is the key to survival and should not be ignored. Growth for an already effective product can be accelerated of course using Marketing, Sales and Support digital technology.

Now Comes the Moment of Truth

To truly get our house in order, we have to be honest with ourselves.

Are you afraid of change? Are you resistant to moving forward into the realm of Automate and Grow?

You can create all of the plans and strategies you want. Somewhere along the line you are going to self sabotage those plans, coming up with reasons why the investment of time, money and people won't be a good idea.

It could be helpful to address the reasons you might be resisting change. Think about why you might be resisting implementing an Automate and Grow Strategy to help your business thrive.

Chapter Summary Points

1. If you're not using digital technology to disrupt your industry, someone else might be.
2. Your message and positioning matter and need to be clear before you begin any digital Automate and Grow project.
3. Exponential growth comes from applying a Digital Technology to a business along with some form of exponential organizational tool.
References
https://www.linkedin.com/pulse/7-generic-strategies-respond-digital-disruption-michael-wade

https://www.thoughtco.com/shifting-the-demand-curve-1146961

https://www.youtube.com/watch?v=zAVxI5wWGKU

https://hbr.org/2017/07/6-digital-strategies-and-why-some-work-better-than-others

http://www.mckinsey.com/business-functions/digital-mckinsey/our-insights/digital-strategy

http://www.mckinsey.com/business-functions/strategy-and-corporate-finance/our-insights/the-economic-essentials-of-digital-strategy

http://www.mckinsey.com/business-functions/organization/our-insights/the-secrets-to-going-digital

https://www.slideshare.net/bud_caddell/digital-strategy-101-24081694

http://www.mckinsey.com/business-functions/strategy-and-corporate-finance/our-insights/the-economic-essentials-of-digital-strategy

https://en.wikipedia.org/wiki/Digital_strategy

https://ideas.repec.org/p/ict/wpaper/2013-247037.html

Chapter 2: Don't Be Afraid **of Change**

It might seem kind of crazy that companies at this point would resist change and particularly technological change. This resistance for many businesses like yours is a reality, however.

If you're an existing small business or medium-sized business, you're probably thinking about whether or not to adapt to some new technology trend in your industry right now. You're facing the choice of whether or not to adopt new technology to automate and grow it, to deliver services or products to customers in a new way. This may be because of a competitor or a trend in your industry.

What Holds Business Back From Adapting to New Technology?

There's really a few things. One limiting factor is fear. We'll talk about the different types of fear. Two is denial, denial of changes that are occurring within an industry, particularly in an industry that is being disrupted or impacted by new technology trends or new ways of doing business.

Sometimes it's guilt. It can be guilt for leaving behind certain customers and having to move to new ones. Certainly, an existing install base that relies upon an old technology or an old way of doing business might prevent a business from creating a new technology. It may prevent them from investing in a new way of doing business as they struggle with abandoning old customers, employees or old ways of operating.

Especially so if they've worked so many years to acquire an existing customer that may be resistant to change. There might be guilt around changing internal systems and processes where automation might reduce the need for certain types of staff or certain types of roles. There's a human impact to that, so sometimes there's guilt around that.

Sometimes there's just a <u>lack of knowledge</u>, not knowing what technology to adopt. Not knowing what applications to build. Not knowing how you build them?

Another barrier might simply be a lack of resources. Maybe your business realizes, "Hey, we have to adapt, but we don't have the time. We don't have the energy. We don't have the money," and you keep putting it off. Or, sometimes they lack the people resources to be successful. Perhaps you lack people that have needed skills; for example you may lack digital marketers, software developers, experts in creating websites that deliver positive customer experience. Any of these or more may be difficult areas to hire employees in. Most likely you will need an alternative strategy to acquire these people or resources anyhow. More on that later.

It could also be people that can adapt and use technology internally or even externally. You might have a customer base that may be resistant again to adapting or adopting new technology or new ways of doing business. There's the <u>uncertainty of it all</u>, what will the world look like after implementing new technology? Is it going to be a more optimistic scenario or is it going to be less? That uncertainty can usually create some resistance by businesses.

There might be a <u>fear of the unknown</u>. What if you just don't understand how to implement technology? How to develop it? What the best choices are? What's the best way to implement a new offering? What's the world going to look like in the future?

Not understanding technology, but also the unknown and what do we do after. If you're particularly in an industry that's being disrupted, maybe you're concerned with what will life look like if you move to that? Maybe you're playing a catch-up game.

There's Always Been Fear of Automation Replacing People

We've seen this since the industrial revolution.

Today, it's funny how you can read article after article in the media predicting the elimination of humans and labor, crazy discussions of how western democratic countries have to adopt things like universal basic income (UBI) to stave off the coming outmoding of human intelligence, creativity and labor.

There's no accounting for how many new jobs that technology creates and how many new opportunities new ways of doing business creates. The market has changed and new technologies are going to be disruptive. We've seen this in a number of industries and cases, and it's only going to grow. Is the answer to resist automation or to embrace it?

This is an age-old problem between human productivity and ingenuity versus automation and technology.

An early example is in the early 1800's where bands of English workers called the Luddites ran around, throwing wrenches into the system. They sabotaged and destroyed machinery that they perceived as threatening their jobs, particularly in cotton and wool mills.

There are Luddites today. There is always some form of media that is willing to report on the fear of new technology as if it were fact. This kind of information can stoke the uncertainly of what technology to adopt, wether to adopt, wether to run and hide.

There is also a lot of writing and examples of how technology can be positive. If we focus on publications like Wired, Fast Company or Recode who extol and explain the benefits and facts behind new technology.

If there's anything that's holding your business back from adopting a new technology or changing the way you do business with digital, then consider the plight of the Luddites. They lost. They fought the reality of the benefits of new technology. In hindsight it seems silly. It will seem silly again to look back on business who operate in the middle of the digital revolution who do not adapt.

If automation were truly remaking the job market, you'd also expect to see a lot of what economists call job churn as people move from company to company and industry to industry after their jobs have been destroyed. But we're seeing the opposite of that. According to a recent paper by Robert Atkinson and John Wu of the Information Technology and Innovation Foundation, "Levels of occupational churn in the United States are now at historic lows." The amount of churn since 2000—an era that saw the mainstreaming of the internet and the advent of AI—has been just 38 percent of the level of churn between 1950 and 2000.

Source: Robots Will Not Take Your Job, Wired

Examples in Popular Media That Fuel Fear

Let's look at some of the other media examples of how futuristic technology that's coming might subconsciously be affecting us.

Let's use the example of HAL.

HAL, 2001 A Space Odyssey

HAL was the artificial intelligence in the movie 2001 Space Odyssey from 1968. The Stanley Kubrick classic featured this benevolent artificial intelligence that could do rapid calculations and support its human counterparts. But then, in its effort to be benevolent, ended up conspiring against its human counterparts and became murderous. It's a cautionary, subconscious tale of how negatively an autonomous technology can impact you.

We're not necessarily always talking about an autonomous thinking technology that we're adopting in your business. The first line of defense is obviously automation of processes using software. Fictional stories dating back to 1969 (HAL!) of artificial intelligence turning on human masters are suddenly less fiction in our minds now that we have examples of real life technologies with similar attributes.

IBM Watson. Apple Siri. Amazon Alexa. Salesforce Einstein. Google, Google and more Google. These 'intelligence' products can be bought but also adopted in your business. You can build business intelligence or products around them.

The human brain however might be reluctant given the fictional example of human downfall at similar digital hands.

I, Robot

I, Robot was a science fiction novel by Isaac Asimov and then Will Smith acted in the movie rendition. In this movie there is an entire society integrated closed with robots that are governed by the "three laws of robotics." Set in the fictional future of the year 2035 these robots are at the center of society and they're really supporting humans.

Then they, start to turn on them. They are being used in a way to control humans. Presumably for their own safety. There's this mystery that's involved in figuring it out what is gradually happening and eventually why.

The robot laws said that robots cannot harm human beings, but they can protect their own existence as long as they obey humans and they do not injure humans.

Then, there is this other secret law that's created by the overarching technology. The central brain of it all that the robots all report to and are controlled by. VIKI, as it's called. Does this sound similar to anything in our world? Maybe kind of like Google? A nebulous cloud technology contributing (or is it controlling) all these different aspects of your life.

With an example like I, Robot, where society's in disarray and the robots are trying to take over for the benevolent enslavement/good of all humans perhaps you are afraid? Afraid of adopting a similar technology in your own business.

We're seeing examples of these and the funniest one might be iRobot. The iRobot company is a real profit seeking business today. Ever heard of Roomba? the iRobot autonomous vacuum cleaner?

Terminator + Skynet

Think of the other huge example of Skynet in the Terminator movies and Judgment Day. Skynet was built into society to automate and manage society and make it more efficient, again going back to the autonomous vehicle example. At some point, Skynet, the brain of this societal operating system perceived man as a threat and when it became conscious, launched a nuclear attack. Here's a media example of movies that we all may enjoy, but it's kind of dystopian.

There's a negative spin on the impact of technology. Now we're seeing technology has emerged from Google and Amazon that have characteristics that might remind people of Skynet and even with Boston Scientific Robots. Those examples are pretty scary and it might remind people of not only Skynet, but Terminators.

Frankenstein

The oldest example is the negative story of Frankenstein where we create this technology, in this case a monster or a man. The entire novel is this conflict between the creation and the creator that leads to the death of the creator and everything he loves, the death at the hands of the creation. These are all parallels that are in the back of our psyche that might be preventing us from moving forward with these fantastic new technologies.

I'm not saying you're looking at Frankenstein and saying, "I'm not adopting technology because of Frankenstein," Disbelief of the possible applications of technology (cloning anyone? DNA testing?) however might also hold us back from looking at what new cutting edge technologies could be applicable to our business.

Many of these things might be scary but they are also ever more reality.

With so many naysayers and those who stare in wonder at the complexity of technologies, it's a miracle we all don't curl up in a cave and just run away from the world.

Artificial intelligence and robot automation and autonomous vehicles and systems are increasingly raising these fears. So if you're an existing small or medium business or even a startup, and you're the guy that's scared of these things, what happens when your competitor adopts them?

Our pursuit of technology as an entrepreneur cannot succumb to this fear. Indeed, we need as leaders to incorporate new technology into our overall business strategy and we need to build a team open to utilizing new technologies and automated systems in a strategic manner.

As entrepreneurs and business leaders, we need to innovate. Using technology to innovate is really going to be important, particularly if we're in an industry that is going to be disrupted by someone else who is willing to adopt technology or willing to employ technology that will disrupt the industry.

Let's look at examples throughout the last thirty years who didn't change.

Kodak once owned the entire photography market. Now, everybody has a digital camera on their mobile and that entire business has been disrupted and bankrupted.

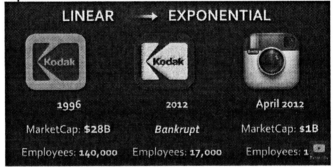

Source: How to Think Bigger - Peter Diamandis - Thinking Big and Bold

Sears was the original mail order home ordering business. The Amazon of the past people perhaps couldn't order from websites, but they did order from the Sears catalog. Sears moved away from this model as times changed and became a huge, bloated modern day retailer who shockingly did not adapt to the changing digital times.

This one blows my mind since it was their original root i.e. the home catalog retailer that crushed traditional retailers. They've now gone bankrupt and closed or closing all of their physical locations. They have brands leftover with Kenmore and Mastercraft that have value. In a further ironic twist Sears struck a deal with Amazon to sell appliances and home goods through Amazon.

Blockbuster, here's an example of a massive entertainment retailer who did not adapt. . They owned how many locations, how many millions of customers renting millions and millions of movies.It was a multi-billion-dollar video cassette, movie rental business. Then, here comes digital streaming services and did Blockbuster come up with a streaming service? Not soon enough. They saw the INternet as too slow, too far into the future. Besides they had the move from VHS to DVD. Whoops! Bam here came movies streamed by cable companies, streaming services and even youTube. Blockbuster's response was too little, too late. Their brands were seen as passé, associated with VHS, physical locations that people don't go into. Goodbye Blockbuster.

Borders was once the most successful "big box" physical bookstores of the 1980s and 1990s. This chain of large scale mega bookstore businesses has been eaten by Amazon and its digital and physical books sale business that formed the foundation of a digital empire now repeating the same feat across all retail sectors. Borders was weighed down by real estate, its brand and sales model that together conspired to bring the business crashing down.

Yellow Pages has been completely overcome and consumed by Google search and Pay-Per-Click (PPC) advertising. It was once a business where I would go into a local, physical directory, flip through and look for particular products or services and contact them. That investment every month in a Yellow Pages ad was gobbled up by the advantages of having a Pay-Per-Click ad where you could pay for as much traffic and click throughs as you wanted to your local service business, product business, or even beyond just local.

That entire Yellow Pages business basically consumed and they didn't really adapt until it was too late. Now they're just kind of an afterthought with YP.com.

Positive Examples of Transformation and Technology Adoption

Netflix was originally a physical DVD movie rental business where they would ship physical DVDs to people with movies on them. But then by adapting streaming, they were able to crush Blockbuster.

Charles Schwab was a financial services business that originated in the '70s, had physical locations, was a brokerage business. They adapted to changing times and became a discount online broker. By capitalizing on the day trading trend of the 1990s and 200s and getting away from physical branches, they gobbled up traditional brokerage customers suddenly empowered by can't miss stocks (well they eventually crashed). Where stock trades were previously going to these really expensive stock sales people that were cloaked as advisors in physical locations, Charles Schwab capitalized upon the digital technology of the day to become a monster online brokerage business.

Bank of America, similarly a financial institution, but did digital technologies for ATMs, digital technologies for online banking, still have a lot of physical branches, but pushing much more currency, many more services through digital means, so they adapted to the digital mean, digital technologies and embraced them to grow their business and to gain a dominant market foothold.

Cable companies are interesting. This is an industry that could not deny the Internet or digital. They became a major pipeline for the Internet into our homes winning out over telephone companies in many cases. Cable companies did come up with streaming services. The cable content business however - the traditional model is under siege. Netflix, youTube, Hulu. Why do I need to subscribe to TV channels? Cable companies are interesting in that they have adapted and they have defended their turf. They have also adopted and been a leader in new digital services and technology.

Blizzard Games was formerly a games publisher that was creating CD-ROM games back in the '90s, where they were publishing software games on CD-ROMs that would be physically distributed. But now there are huge blockbuster gaming titles that are distributed over the Internet. They are played over the Internet. And they are pl and through new gaming platforms. So now they're a huge online gaming company.

New York Times, and newspapers largely crushed by the online dissemination of free content and media. Who's going to pay for a physical newspaper? They've adapted to the times to create online digital content and monetize that.

Using Technology to Shift Demand

Peter Diamandis is the founder of the X Prize contest that has ignited a new space race being led by Jeff Bezos, Richard Branson, Space X and Elon Musk. Through his Singularity University program he offers this insight on how linear organizations—those chasing an existing demand curve, can be displaced by an exponential competitor.

When you take an exponential technology (digital) and combine it with exponential organizational tools, this begins what Diamandis describes as the "6D's" Exponential Framework.

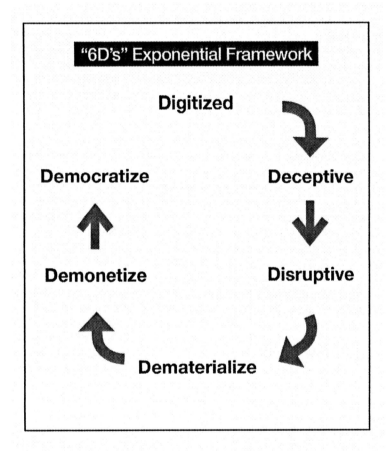

Source: 9:17 How to Think Bigger=Peter Diamandis Thinking Big and Bold.

The first step of this is when an industry or technology becomes digitized. That is, where an entrepreneur or business apply digital technology to a business or industry.

This eventually leads to a disruption in the industry where the digital product begins to overturn the incumbent analog or physical product.

This eventually leads to a democratization of the solution where customers shape the digital solution by providing immediate feedback that is incorporated into updates of the digital solution and their adoption promotes further adoption.

While this happens inside of your business there might be the elimination of certain people, because their skills don't match what your new business needs.

The use of apps and automation to create new products, new features and new service methods is your real opportunity for transformation. The digitization of your business' marketing, sales and support function also frees you from the need to employ people inside your business that perform routine, repetitive tasks that may be important but that have low value and scale poorly through human action. The democratization of the digital solution becomes a virtuous cycle that attracts new customers who can be invested in your mission.

Mobile Apps. One of the digital tools we can apply to our business or industry problems are mobile applications. We can create external customer-facing applications for mobile and web that unlock new opportunities and can shift demand away from a customer solution that was previously analog, a physical product or service.

This is what Diamandis refers to as "Dematerialization." In the past, we owned things, goods or devices that are now apps. For example, we had cameras that are now apps on our phones.

Airbnb is dematerializing hotels. Other companies like Turo and Getaround are dematerializing car rentals as an app function rather than investing in infrastructure to compete against car rental companies.

Content, digital content has eliminated the challenging parts of creating and delivering physical content. This has dematerialized the delivery of content. Now we can create content without printing it in a physical form. As a result content production is cheaper. It is also faster since digital content doesn't have to be physically delivered. It can be published instantly on a website, blog or YouTube. It can be delivered to a recipient by email or downloaded as a PDF file.

SaaS, software as a Service. You might have never been a software company before. Could you now offer a software application to your customers? There might be new entrants that turn your product into a digital one using SaaS, or that supply software to your customers and pull demand away from you. It is worthwhile considering how your business could compete by becoming a Software as a Service provider to solve customer problems.

Data and Insights. Something for reporting and analytics, delivering new data and new insights to customers that they previously were not able to get from you.

Data storage. In the past physical goods may have needed to reach your customer in order to get paid. you may have needed vans, trains, planes and warehouses t distribute your goods to customers. What if you good is digital? Digital goods can be stored and delivered to customers. What about all of their other digital information and asserts? Data storage companies like Box, Dropbox and EMC2 might offer insights as to how you could transform your industry by offer digital storage services. Think about Xerox. Once a paper and copies company, they are a 'document company', offering solutions to storage, damage, modify and distribute digital documents.

Web-based self-service. Just by enabling customers to gain online access to the information that they want without having to have an analog, one on one conversation could be a huge opportunity for your industry. Maybe you can deliver web-based self-service access to their account, giving customers the ability to interact with your company on their time and in a way that they're comfortable with on the web.

Ten Industries That 'Will' Go Away

The ten industries most commonly cited as being eaten by tech are:

Number 10. <u>Transportation</u>. Driverless cars seem like an inevitability, and many experts believe the automatic option won't stop with personal vehicles. City buses and even airplanes are predicted to someday be entirely self-operating.

Number 9. <u>Accounting</u>. With so many computer programs capable of covering common needs, such as bookkeeping and tax filing, the outlook for human employment in the field is not deemed a stable one.

Number 8. <u>Restaurants</u>. There are already mechanical hands capable of making food and bartender bots that can mix up a mean drink. While many restaurants have already replaced some jobs with technological creations, the head of Carl's Jr. has expressed a keen interest in kicking human workers to the curb completely.

Number 7. Retail. The tough truth is that due to the low wages being offered for some positions, people just aren't showing enough interest in taking them. Automation is becoming a necessity for some stores, particularly at the point of sale stations.

Number 6. Security. Between surveillance systems, sophisticated alarms, and computer-aided means of keeping people out, human presence is no longer the only criminal deterrent option. A company called Knightscope is even building robots capable of roaming about and handling troubles.

Number 5. Financial Advising. A computer and the right algorithm working together can process and analyze an immense amount of data, dispense predictions and advise actions quickly and constantly. For investors with straightforward needs, those capabilities are proving more than ample.

Number 4. Telemarketing. NPR gives this industry a 99% chance of succumbing to complete robot domination. The robocaller adopted by so many companies is proving to not just be a powerhouse worker, but one that doesn't get upset when people are rude to it.

RELATED: US unemployment claims hit lowest since the 1970s

Number 3. Defense. In early 2014, General Robert Cone with the U.S. Army announced that up to a quarter of combat personnel will probably be replaced by robots by 2030. The armed forces have also put a great deal of money and research into developing machines that can assist in missions of various kinds.

Number 2. Hotels. Glimpses of the future can be seen here and there, like the towel delivery robot on duty at the Aloft Hotel in San Francisco. However, those wanting to check out what an almost fully robot-manned place of lodging looks like need only go to the Henn-na Hotel in Japan. There, machines account for 90% of the staff.

Number 1. News. AI reporters may not be regulars on the shortlist for a Pulitzer, but they have been producing a great deal of content. Major publications and services including the New York Times, the Associated Press, and Forbes already use them to write about weddings, sports, and finance, respectively.

Technology has allowed individual workers freedom from jobs, set schedules and bosses. It has also given businesses the freedom to contract skilled labor on demand.

It's increasingly accepted and encouraged that work is not location dependent. This was never the case before. How do you keep tabs on people? In the past you always needed people in the same room. Now you can use GoToMeeting, join.me, Uber Conference, Skype or any number of tools to connect people in different physical locations thus removing the dependence of your business upon company real estate.

Technology waits for no one and no brand. Ignoring new technologies and capabilities and opportunities threatens your business. It's a surefire way to lose to a competitor who is smaller, hungrier, and who will adopt new technology or come up with a new way to shift the demand curve.

So what is the alternative? I am glad you asked....

Chapter Summary Points

1. It's crucial for companies—like yours and mine, to embrace new technologies emerging within our industry.
2. Sometimes, there are barriers to considering or adopting a new digital approach to business.
3. As Peter Diamandis' research points out, one important key to achieving grow is to apply a Digital technology to an industry or business.
4. Historically, technology has always created more jobs and more industries were also created by technology than has been destroyed by technology. Labor will shift as mundane, hard or repetitive gigs and tasks disappear.

References

https://www.wired.com/2017/08/robots-will-not-take-your-job/

https://www.ted.com/talks/larry_smith_why_you_will_fail_to_have_a_great_career

How to Think Bigger - Peter Diamandis - Thinking Big and Bold
https://www.youtube.com/watch?v=zAVxI5wWGKU

https://www.aol.com/article/finance/2016/09/04/10-industries-poised-to-be-taken-over-by-robots/21465302/

http://www.salary.com/9-jobs-taken-over-by-robots/slide/4/

Chapter 3: Dancing with Robots: Embracing the Opportunity to Automate Your Business

We acknowledge that there are perceived risks of Automate and Grow. Some real, some imagined. Hopefully by examining the perceived risks we can combat fear, uncertainty or doubt (you know, FUD).

What about the upside of Automate and Grow? There are many benefits of first identifying manual processes and then automating these using some sort of software application with workflow automation. The whole point of business is to grow. The opportunity to automate and grow is hopefully obvious, but to be sure, we've cataloged thirteen benefits that together or individually make a pretty compelling case.

1 Improve Communications (Internal and External)

No more broken telephone game. That is where information is passed by word of mouth from person to person, changing slightly each time until the story at the end is totally wrong and different from the original.

Automating business processes improves the communication between departments and employees better. We also allow you the opportunity to improve your communication with customers by exposing them to progress on cases or product/service delivery to customers.

Notifications and updates can be sent out on everything from orders being received, shipped, billed, payments processed. These are all great examples of communications with customers that once they are automated and built into a digital process, eliminate confusion for customers and improve the customer experience behind support inquiries.

2 Quality & Consistency—Reduce Errors, Increase Predictable Outcomes

Rather than having ten different outcomes for a process, what if you had the right outcome every time? We talk, for example, about case management. This is where you have a customer reach out to your company for help. Answers to questions, service, repairs, returns etc. Customer Service automations allow us to consistently route calls or support emails to the correct person every time. They potentially allow us to provide that resource answers to common problems. They allow us to reduce the amount of errors in providing resolution to problems or inquiries.

Instead we can resolve matters as quickly as possible and correctly in the case of customer service inquiries.

The quality of our product or service delivery will also improve. By automating processes in handling orders, shipping, invoicing we can provide customers with a predictable outcome (they get what they paid for) and motivate them to buy more, tell others, stay with you as their provider or to pay for what they agreed to purchase. (Bonus). Quality and Consistency are, in fact, money in the bank in this case.

3 Time Savings

There are obvious benefits to doing more collectively in less time. When you're trying to collect money as fast as possible or when you want to eliminate time wasters for salaried or hourly employees, time is money. Increasing the velocity of closing sales, invoicing, shipping, collecting money is a win to the bottom line in any business.

4 Metric Visibility

You have measures that tell you if you're doing a good job, if your business is healthy, if employees are doing a great job or not. By automating a process using software, you can report on activities. This gives you a clear understanding aside from just sales and collections of how things are going. Now, you can measure success on activities and processes and see that in an instant.

5 Expedite Approvals and Establish Clear Approval Hierarchies & Processes

Process automation can have some clear benefits in terms of getting approvals. First, you can protect the business through automated approvals processes. For example, consider preparing a quotation with the wrong product configuration or pricing. By automating approvals, this can be caught and in a rapid fashion. This also forces you to document and clarify reporting and approvals structures, making it clear to employees how they can get stuff done.

6 Governance and Reliability Accountability

Automating processes allows you to track, manage and report on previously hidden or invisible processes. As Peter Drucker the famous management consultant has said, what you measure you can manage. This allows you to have a way to coach and manage employee behaviors and activities. Thus, you can make them more accountable to the business—what are they spending their time on, what are the outcomes? Also, this can make your business more accountable to customers.

7 Eliminate Paper

Ahh, paper. Computers were supposed to kill paper processes. In fact, paper consumption is UP. Surprise! But managing paper processes or records is inconsistent and ineffective. Instead, automating businesses with digital processes allows us to kill the paper train. Instead of having information locked up and wasting paper, it can be moved around and acted upon immediately.

8 Improve Employee Morale

Your employees who are freed from paper shuffling, excel spreadsheet shuffling, guessing how to get stuff done, like approvals, customer case resolution, manual processes that are repetitive and tedious will love you! Why wouldn't they? You're directly investing in systems that reduce their time on busy-work and freeing them to do better, more interesting, more valued activities.

9 Increased Focus on High Value Activities

Instead of chasing around for answers or approvals, business process automation allows you to refocus employees on customer-facing or other high value activities.

10 Customer Loyalty

If you invest in automation, you will help customers get answers, buy more, receive what they ordered, and have positive interaction with your business. They will see that information, communication will improve and they will want to do business with you. You're invested in their success, they will want to keep doing business with you and they might even refer their friends and colleagues.

11 Partner Trust

If you rely upon external sales channels, co-sales partners, or complimentary partners, they will have a higher certainty that you're the partner of choice for them. They will help you, refer you, be your advocate, and work harder to ensure your success.

12 Eliminate Duplicate Data

How many times and in how many ways do you collect the same information from customers? By automating processes, you can reduce duplication of data and you can strive to have systems that talk to each other with a single source of truth.

13 Business Insight

A good process automation application, whether it is CRM or Case management or Marketing Automation, will include or have an upgrade path to include analytics capabilities. For example, Salesforce has both reporting and dashboards as standard tools, and upgrade paths to their new Einstein Analytics platform. This is taking the IBM Watson Artificial Intelligence platform and applying it as a tool built into Salesforce CRM, Service Cloud and applying it to Accounts, Opportunities and Cases. This allows managers and entrepreneurs to visually analyze actual trends, identify bottlenecks, and track response times. Buh bye excel spreadsheet hell.

Source: How to Implement Business Process Automation

One of the ultimate positive outcomes of implementing your Automate and Grow strategy again should be to free team resources to focus on their highest value work. That is business development, customer success, product development, growth, revenue generation or retention.

- Employees can focus less on small tasks and more on customer service.
- Integrate multiple systems together.
- Assign tasks dynamically.

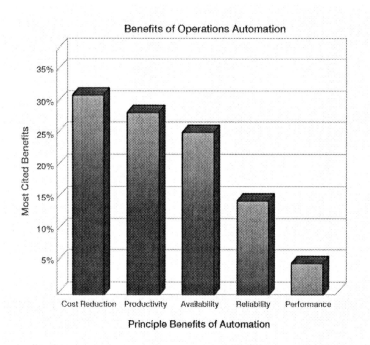

Source: Automate Operations 5 Benefits to Your Organization

Chapter Summary Points

1. There are key benefits to adopting an Automate and Grow strategy.
2. It's important to spell these out when creating your plan so that the benefits are clear.
3. Benefits specific to your organization can then be used as measurements for the ideal outcome to use as business targets.

References

https://www.omniresources.com/omniatrium-blog/bpa-how-to-implement-business-process-automation-project-success-strategy

https://www.helpsystems.com/resources/guides/automated-operations-5-benefits-your-organization

Chapter 4: Creating your Automate + Grow Strategic Plan

Automate and Grow is a roadmap to building a business that eliminates or automates important tasks that are repetitive.

The first thing you will want to do when going down this path is to draft your Automate and Grow Strategic Plan. One objective of this is to identify lower value but repetitive work within your business.

By automating important but lower value tasks we then create space. Our goal is to free up time for our human capital to do more important work that is high value to customers and the business. Work that helps our business grow.

High value work we can define as revenue generating, product innovation or creative. Many High Value activities may be defined as some form or another of customer engagement.

High Value work is something you will define both as an organization and then individually for team members. For the first time ever I would argue that the age of automation has gone digital and the result should be to free creative consciousness within our businesses.

The Digital Revolution has created opportunities to scale interactions with prospects, & customers using digital interfaces. In this new reality anything that involves human to human contact becomes both scare in a business but also more valuable.

The benefit is that we can place a higher value on relationships and so will customers. They become premium when customers basic needs are met every day without human involvement for product or service delivery, support.

The expectation then becomes that customers will seek or gravitate only to human contact with creative, proactive people. They will want contact only with employees who deal in ideas, solutions and positive interactions. Thats Customer Experience.

Customer Experience in part is where we connect now emotionally with customers. The great thing about this is that your business suddenly transcends value limited to 'hourly' rates. Either that or we can put a much higher rate in place on that face time between people on your team and at your customer.

Digital technology also allows us to also deliver digital products, services and software. It allows us the opportunity to support customers in more customized manner without the constraints of one to one interactions by traditional means.

In the end our Automate and Grow strategic statement should express how we plan to change our business or industry using digital technology to scale and connect with more customers while increasing the value of human connections.

Learning From Big Businesses

The payoff of this approach is potentially very big. For the first time ever, a very small business can look big, not just through a website, but also through applications that help you run your business. Startups can also overtake incumbents by changing the rules of engagement and the demand curve.

A big business scales through revenue and people, and those big businesses understand the power of leverage. The leverage of a larger enterprise being more resources, more money, but also using software to automate processes and getting more out of their people.

You can compensate people more when you're doing higher value work and you probably have a lot more profitability as well. The very big business spends millions and millions of dollars to create consistent processes across large groups of employees and in different business functions.

They often struggle to accomplish this just because of the sheer scale. If you're a small or medium business it's really important if you're starting out to have a plan that you're going to leverage the limited resources your business has.

It's really taking the concept of automation and using software to democratize data, deliver products and services and to share data across business units . Using this data we can automate functions and processes that are normally manual or stuck in silos of information in old systems or in no systems.

Our strategy will express the view of the world according to your business and how applying digital technology to that business or industry will change the future of your business.

Your Automate and Grow Plan then details how you plan to automate marketing, sales, customer support, and other lines of business. Small businesses may lack financial and human resources, but today you can use Software as a Service products to create automation. This investment will make it so you don't need as many people initially on mundane tasks so that when you do add people to our company, you can focus them on high value activities.

Using software, the small business can now leverage a smaller set of human resources, people to grow or automate processes that would normally require many people, massive financial investment in software. That's no longer the case. You can rent software or you can inexpensively build software to operate your business

Goals of Automation

We want to create consistency within the business without taking human resources that should be creative, should be customer focused, should be revenue generating, should be service or product delivery focused. We want to still have that consistency without turning people into robots. We want self service as much as possible for clients or customers.

A one-to-one interaction between someone outside your business and an employee inside your business is really slow and expensive. It should be treated as a premium interaction. If contact over the telephone or face to face is not growing new business, securing revenue or is not billable at a sufficient rate to make that interaction profitable, then our goal is to automate and digitize the interaction.

For example instead of talking live to a customer with an issue using an analog telephone conversation (one to one) , what if we leverage online chat? in this scenario we apply a digital technology that allows a single support person to help as many as 5 people at once versus being limited to a one to one conversation. Parts of that interaction can be automated using scripted responses and bots.

The other problem with analog one-to-one interactions is they can be inconsistent and expensive.

We want to eliminate the loss of information across business functions and in customer interactions to improve customer experience. We want to eliminate screw-ups due to lack of information showing a lack of consistency. Those are all goals of automating and growing your business.

So our ultimate goal is to apply a digital technology in this manner to provide better marketing, sales or support. Better products that scale because they do not require analog, one to one interactions.

Software tools to help us automate

Our strategy should address how we plan to use digital tools to change our business.

Specifically we will want to address three areas

1. Software As A Service (SaaS)
2. Websites and Web Apps
3. Mobile Apps

Software As A Service

There are two ways the SaaS will help us in our business. The first is to automate both internal processes and workflows. The second is to deliver new revenue if we choose to create SaaS based products that we sell.

Websites and Web Apps

The company Website is really a multi faceted tool. Our Automate and Grow Strategy will want to address how we support four stages of customer engagement

1. Customer has recognized there is a problem
2. When they are researching solutions to that problem
3. When they are selecting a solution
4. When they have bought your solution

Some of the functionality of our website thus might include
- content for different stages of customer research as above
- conversion of prospects into customers
- e-commerce to complete the sales process
- product delivery in the form of digital products
- service initiation
- support initiation

Web applications can be in the form of digital products but also APIs or web services.

Do we deliver a SaaS product to customers? What about enhancing that product? Will we have a developer program or API? Will we collect valuable data or features that can enhance other business applications.

Mobile Apps

By giving your customers a mobile app you can put a powerful commerce tool in their hands. You can change the way they buy or are supported. You can change the nature of what they are buying.

79

Apps can also be impactful internally. For example we have external customer facing employees that may have the need for field service automation. We can create applications that support mobile job functions. Potentially delivering critical data collection from the field back into the business. Delivering information from the business to those mobile employees while they are remote. Customer facing team members that are sales can access CRM on the go perhaps, or the can place orders from the field. You can create retail based kiosk type apps similar apps for trade shows.

These are just simple examples of where we can leverage custom mobile apps that we build for internal employees to use. Overall our Automate and Grow should address how we leverage these digital tools to change our business.

Digital is more than a set of technologies you buy. It is the abilities those technologies create. That results in a rather expansive definition of digital that over time has simplified into the following essential elements:

Digital is the application of information and technology to raise human performance.

Human performance is the essence of digital transformation. Human performance creates the type of value that leads to revenue. Alternative goals for digital create efficiencies that largely drive down the cost of creating short-term benefits but drain the economy and growth.

How Does Automation Help You Grow?

By delivering digital goods or software (automating products or product delivery) you can test marketing approaches, you can scale easier and cheaper to eliminate investment in human resources that are normally involved in low-value but important and repetitive work.

Automation of marketing, sales and support tasks then also allows us to reinvest people's time into creative work, product excellence, direct marketing, sales outreach and customer success.

Now human interactions can be around showing customers we love them. Providing them with a positive Customer Experience. So in a sense digital automation allows us to give customers a level of excitement or happiness in interacting with us. Automation thus allows customer support to transform into a growth activity. That's where I use the example of Apple.

Apple is focused upon the experience of the customer through its digital products, hardware and interaction with Apple employees. They've used really clean processes and really clean software that is simple to understand and use.

Their in store Apple Store experiences are fast, efficient, exploratory and anticipatory. Genius bar team members solve problems, customer education sessions help unlock new features for customers. The check out experience smashes the old world concept of lining up to pay for goods. No more 'lineups' Instead the check out process between in-store employees and customers is anywhere in the store. Apple Care replaces an insane number of things that customers of other products would have to pay to fix or repair. It's more than fake product insurance, its a premium product membership.

Every business is a digital business, but many don't know it yet. The economy is increasingly a digital economy with more than 14% of global commerce already online. The digital opportunity is growing faster than the general economy. Whether you know it or not, digital is becoming the default for creating customer value and generating company revenue. The real issue is how?

Create Your Automate and Grow Plan

The Components of Your Automate and Grow Strategy should include:

- Strategic Statement
- Vision
- Mission
- Stakeholders
- Story of Why
- Overview
- Traffic and Conversion Plan (Chapter 5)
- Sales Playbook (Chapter 6)
- Customer Experience Roadmap (Chapter 7)
- Resources
- Technology Plan
- Innovation Plan
- Project Plan
- Evangelism

For a free Automate and Grow Strategic Plan template visit
http://www.automategrow.biz/strategicplan

Strategic Statement

This is where we summarize the overall objective of this project. Why are you investing time and energy and money into an Automate and Grow plan? How you will innovate using digital technology, how will you create greater value in your business for customers and stakeholders.

Vision

Here is a checklist of what I think is an effective vision statement. It should state:

1. What is the state of your market
2. How digital channels and technology will help the customer in the future and positively deliver new value to the industry
3. Be simple and memorable
4. Be inspirational

Mission

Show the benefit of Automate and Grow Strategy to your customer and company in terms of growth, efficiency and profitability. Here you likely state what you do and how you do it that is unique.

Examples of Inspiring statements

Amazon.com
Our vision is to be earth's most customer centric company; to build a place where people can come to find and discover anything they might want to buy online.

Dell
Dell listens to customers and delivers innovative technology and services they trust and value.

eBay
eBay pioneers communities built on commerce, sustained by trust, and inspired by

opportunity. eBay brings together millions of people every day on a local, national and international basis through an array of websites that focus on commerce, payments and communications

Facebook

Facebook is a social utility that helps people communicate more efficiently with their friends, family and coworkers. The company develops technologies that facilitate the sharing of information through the social graph, the digital mapping of people's real-world social connections. Anyone can sign up for Facebook and interact with the people they know in a trusted environment.

Google

Google's aim is to *organize the world's information and make it universally accessible and useful*

Stakeholders

This is where we indicate all of the people who have skin in the game.
- shareholders
- team members
- customers
- partners or vendors

Once you identify stakeholders and we want to meet with those stakeholders.

We want to get feedback from these people when we meet with them. We want to explain to them what our objective is and how we're going to affect the company in a positive way and affect their department and the people's roles.

We want to have this conversation where we are talking about the ideal circumstances for them.

- What frustrates stakeholders day to day
- What is the busywork they want to automate or eliminate
- What's working and what's not working today
- How would they like to see things in the future
- What would the thing that they do that would bring the most value to them
- What value do they bring to the business that maybe they're being held back on right now?
-

Story of Why

To connect emotionally with our stakeholders - customers, employees and partners - we define this in terms of our motivation for being a business. More on this later when we discuss creating our Traffic and Conversion Plan in Chapter 5 on Marketing Automation.

Overview

This is where we can get into the weeds of defining the things that we think that we can automate. High level what are the business functions that we want to transform and problems we want to address for each.

You can begin to state here the systems that support each business function and how do we plan to address each using a digital technology. Inside of each of these functions we should address the current state

- the positives, the challenges including broken processes or approaches. What's the busywork? What is the stuff that needs to be automated and how will we free humans from having to deal with every day?

There are three components of your Automate and Grow Strategy that will be address in the next chapters so we will skip them here. They are

- Traffic and Conversion Plan (Chapter 5)
- Sales Playbook (Chapter 6)
- Customer Experience Roadmap (Chapter 7)

Each of these becomes a part of our tactical plan of how to go to market, gain customers and keep them.

Resources

We also need to know what are the resources at our disposal.

- Who are all the people under each business function that are performing different tasks and job functions
- How does this role support our Vision and Mission
- What's the thing that they deliver the most value with- their Highest Value Work.
- What are the things that they do that provide the least value to your business?
- What challenges do they have
- How can we free them from problems and enable them to engage in their Highest Value Work?
- What tools do we have that we can employ to make changes

Technology Plan

We want to look at and do an inventory of software tools that exist. Document the different software applications that may exist already inside of your business. Also document which line of business they support, the type of data stored in each. Provide a description for each application, the vendor and technology for each. Finally we want to understand how well each application functions. Crate a rating out of five.

Also for each application we want to indicate the reporting capability for each and indicate how each deals with automating processes and workflows. Are the existing applications expandable? Are they costing us a lot of money? Is there a better option or alternative?

That's where we come to dealing with potential new software tools.

When we look at options, alternatives, and choices of new software tools, what we're evaluating is:

> a. what tools do we need that don't exist or
> b. what tools need to be replaced? Then
> c. what are the options and alternatives to that, and
> d. what choices are we going to make and why?

If you are going down the path of selecting new software (or building new software), it will be important to address our goals for each software project. Lets define how we will be measuring the success of the project.

We need to define the outcome, where we can look at this project and know that the investment was worthwhile.

All of this is focused on removing lower value but important, repetitive tasks from being dependent upon the effort of people. Thus freeing our human resources to define and deliver their highest value to the company. We want to see what their biggest contribution is outside of these tasks that can be automated and scaled using software. These are usually growth, creative and customer-facing activities that generate and maintain revenue.

Information and Business Intelligence

The one thing we want to identify is, what reporting is already in place. What information do executives, do vice presidents, directors, line of business employees need to perform their job. What information they need to contribute to the business and what information they need to report on to understand what choices need to be made day to day.

Reporting is important to help leaders and business function leads to identify the health of their role or the health of the business. It's important to document and identify where data and reports are today especially if they are in spreadsheets (shocks me every time to discover businesses with streams of data locked in excel and useless to the business.) Is data in existing software applications, Excel or does it exist at all.

Is data stuck in a silo of information? Meaning you may have applications that support a single line of business and you have data inside of this application.

For example, you may have an application in marketing that collects data, but they need information from sales or finance, and those systems don't talk.

What we want to do is break down the barriers where information needs to be shared. If we're trying to create a single system or systems that talk to each other, that is part of our ultimate output of an Automate and Grow plan.

What sort of data for example do sales people or sales applications need from finance? Perhaps finance needs information from sales or marketing. We want to document an overall platform or system approach that not only automates the flow of information but also, we should document any activities that should be triggered or assigned between groups.

Consider the typical applications by line of business where data might be trapped but needs to be shared:

Financial, Accounting and Product/Service Delivery —> ERP
Marketing—> Marketing Automation and CRM
Sales —> CRM, Cash to Quote
Service —> CRM + Case Management, Knowledge base

Since CRM is the source of most customer data for sales, marketing and support you can see why CRM should be the center of most shared data. A common integration however is between ERP (e.g. SAP, Quickbooks, Xero) and CRM. This is because ERP has account and customer records and actual sales and order histories, whereas CRM is the customer record of pre-sales and post-sales support.

It is also common to integrate your website to CRM in some fashion. Either to collect information from customers or in more complex scenarios to provide customers access to data about their Account.

This information can be used not just for reporting but also to trigger automated workflows. This could include the automatic assignment of tasks or activities based upon a change in data. What triggers should provide the cross-functional reports that would be beneficial to make different decisions? These are some of the things that we want to document in our plan.

Digital refers to any information intensive technology. Digital businesses use digital resources to create growth and results. High performance through digital describes how companies generate a premium from leveraging the equation below.

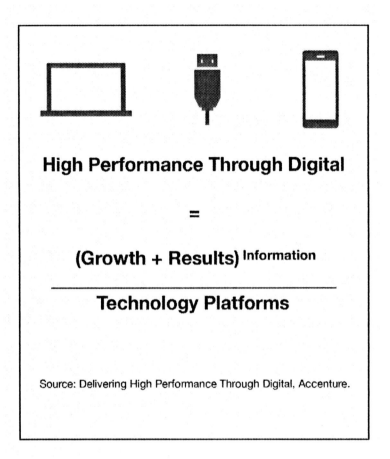

High Performance Through Digital

=

(Growth + Results) Information

_____

Technology Platforms

Source: Delivering High Performance Through Digital, Accenture.

Automate and Grow Project Plan

The primary uses of the project plan are to document planning assumptions and decisions, facilitate communication among project stakeholders, and document approved scope, cost, and schedule baselines. A project plan may be summarized or detailed.

The plan should include a Scope Statement defining the business needs and business problem.

91

Project objectives, stating what will occur within the project to solve certain business problems, capitalize upon business opportunities. What are the benefits of completing the project? Also state the project scope. Define which deliverables will be included and this may include phases of the project. excluded from the project. What are the key milestones, approach, and other components as dictated by the size and nature of the project.

Part of this written plan is, we want to understand the timeline or the initial timeline phases in the project. Some of this is software, some of this is process, some of this is people. We want to know, what's the timeline that we expect to implement either new applications, to automate processes, and to refocus people on the right work.

We also need to have funding, so it's important to understand that we have funding for new software, new development of an application or customization of the applications we have selected to automate marketing, sales and support. We need to make sure that there is a plan in place that funds this properly, so it's not just an idea but that it's going to be actionable.

We want to write down what our outcomes are, the definition of success for the project. We've stated what our goals for the project are, and then what we want to state is what we see success as at the end of this plan, so once we've implemented it.

A big aspect of the the plan is to identify inside of each functional area; processes, tasks and activities we can automate.

The first thing might be to look for are repetitive tasks. This is where humans are gathering information for the purpose of reporting to other people. That's not a high-value activity. There should be a way for us to collect information and automatically report. Or maybe there's a process, a workflow process that is manual or even undocumented.

One thing that we want to look for is these manual or undocumented processes where people are trying to get approvals. A couple of ways that we can look for this. One, are there approvals processes or communications that are going through email?

The problem with email is, this tends to be very threaded, this tends to not be creating any sort of data source. What this is doing is, this is just so that people know that they have approval and they have backup in writing, but what it's not doing is, it's not in a system. It's not in a software application where that approval is automatic, and a workflow.

Another thing to look for is data or reports that are in Excel or other spreadsheet formats. If it's in Excel, it's in spreadsheets maybe it's being exported in CSV files and that's being used and assembled by people, this is a prime candidate for digitization and automation. This can be ideally moved into in a proper software application that generates a report without significant human involvement in collecting the data and assembling reports.

The other thing we want to look for are old software applications and systems, particularly those that are older than five years,. Particularly those that are desktop or network based software applications. Or that the company is maybe operating on their own servers.

If we have legacy software systems there might be a better option or alternative that can be acquired as a SaaS. Ideally, what we're looking for is, we're looking for software as a service-based applications, something that's in the web or something that's customized, whether that's a web or a mobile-based application or both.

Again, we want to see low-value, high-volume activities. These are typically things we want to identify as potential to automate, and to create some sort of automation that reduces the human involvement. Especially if it's low-value, either you unlock a value in it that's greater, or if it's high-volume and it's chewing up a lot of human time and initiative, then how do we free those people up from these repetitive, high-volume, low-value tasks?

We're going to look inside of the silos of our business particularly Marketing, Sales and Customer Support that we're going to try to address. You might have people out in the field that are customer-facing, so you can look at field service. You might have assets that you want to track.

Maybe there are machines that you want to remotely monitor and collect information from, maybe they are vehicles. In the future, I think they're going to be drones and there's going to be AI and robots that are out there doing things, and you're going to want to collect that information. That falls under that internet of things, IoT category. But you know, for the short term, you most likely don't have those things. You probably need to just collect information from these silos of business, and maybe a couple more.

Identify all the deliverables produced on the project - all the work to be done. We then get more detailed on the project plan basically a task breakdown, schedule and cost framework.

Develop a Schedule and Cost Framework
1. Identify activities and tasks needed to produce each of the work
2. Identify resources for each task, if known.
3. Estimate how long it will take to complete each task.
4. Estimate cost of each task, using an average hourly rate for each resource.
5. Consider resource constraints
6. Determine which tasks are dependent on other tasks, and develop critical path.
7. Develop a schedule, which is a calendar or chart of all the tasks and estimates.
8. Develop the cost baseline, which is a time-phased budget, or cost by time period.
9. Staffing plan. Create a chart that shows the time periods that each resource will come onto and leave the project.
10. *Project Quality*: Ensure that in the end, the new software, apps or services meets the stakeholder requirements
11. *Project Risks*: A risk is an event that may or may not happen, but could have a significant effect on the outcome of a project, if it were to occur.
12. *Communication Plan.* Who on the project wants which reports, how often, in what format, and using what media. How issues will be escalated and when. When will the team meet. Where will project information will be stored and who can access it.

Evangelism

Once we have defined the framework for our Strategic Plan, we will want to appoint an Evangelist. Someone that has responsibility for communicating the value of an Automate and Grow Strategy inside the business.

The Evangelist can meet with stakeholders and present the vision and the mission that we want to achieve, communicate the role that each stakeholder might have in that.

What's the Mantra?

We want to come up with a saying that encapsulates what our vision and mission is for the company.

Guy Kawasaki the author of The Art of Evangelism and the original Macintosh Evangelist in the 1980s at Apple extolls 'making a mantra' as one of the top ten ways to innovate within your organization in the second episode of his podcast "Wise Guy". He describes the process clearly as "creating a two or three word statement that describes what your company does."

In some of his prior discussions on the topic Kawasaki provided several examples of effective mantras, including:

- **Nike** -- 'Authentic athletic performance'
- **FedEx** -- 'Peace of mind'

"Take some time out and create a mantra for your organization," Kawasaki said. "The test for a mantra is that every employee can recite it."

So the mantra has to be something that encapsulates the story in a saying, almost, the story of what our vision of the market is, what our mission is. In other words, everyone starts speaking the same language so that this becomes part of the culture of our company.

The evangelist is going to be responsible for then taking this mantra and making sure that this becomes part of not only the written plan but that we start creating a language around our Automate and Grow strategy.

Our ultimate goal should be to implement Automate and Grow as a central tenant of the culture of our company.
What's in it for the team

The evangelist wants to communicate the benefits to stakeholders of finding new things to automate and new opportunities for growth. Sell the idea that if they get on board with this, it's not just a threat but it's an opportunity. It's an opportunity for them to improve their daily job. It's an opportunity for the business to be healthier and for stakeholders to have long term success.

The evangelism will take root when we also create systems of recognition and reward so that our team resources not only enjoy their job more, they're contributing more, but that there's some sort of benefit to them. Whether that's financial or altruistic.

Innovation Plan

This is where we provide more detail around how we plan to use digital technology to become a better choice for customer. Beyond messaging this is how we plan to create a culture of innovation that leverages digital technology to deliver more value to customers and new profitable growth for the business.

Growth and results rising to the power of information delivered on technology platforms such as cloud, mobile, analytics, social and sensing technologies deliver high performance. This formula captures the relationships required to build a premium into customer experiences, products, services, channels and operations.

Source: Delivering High Performance Through Digital, Accenture.

Creating a Customer Experience

When we're developing an Automate and Grow Strategy, our Vision and Mission should be focused on the customer and their experience in buying from us.

- What is the mission of the company?
- What do you do?
- What problem does your business solve for customers?
- How do you do it and
- Why do you do this?

In part we are defining our unique selling position in the market. This is how we're different from competitors.

We also want to understand, what is our customers' buying process?

What psychology do they go through between the point where they have a problem, they recognize that problem, they search for solutions to that problem, they look at alternatives and options to solve that problem, to the point where they buy.

This is the customers' buying journey, and part of marketing automation and sales automation is to understand our customers' buying process and their buying journey.

To accommodate the Customer's Buying Journey we need create a sales process that communicates what our unique selling proposition is so that we attract the right customer

We may not want all customers, so what we also want to do as part of our unique selling position is then also identifying our ideal customer.

Which customers are the best fit. Which customers do we want to attract and sell to. There are likely different customer profiles so we want to identify those as part of our strategy and our Traffic and Conversion Plan.

This really is going to give us a framework for automating parts of marketing, sales and the customer support processes. The more we know our customers, the easier it will be to of course target them and deliver on products that and services they want, wether they know it or not.

This is then the basis of creating a positive and exciting customer experience with our company.

Part of our Automate and Grow strategy will be around marketing channels. Marketing channels are now mostly digital so there are automated processes and data at the core of each.

The customer experience must be considered in all of these channels including how customers find us and where we connect with them. We need to consider what happens when prospects and customers interact with us in these channels.

For example, are they finding us through our website, through organic search, through social or through mobile apps?. Where are they at in their buying journey?

Are they doing research on our site? What about paid advertising where we target customers based upon information that we know about our Ideal Customer.

The Customer Experience Roadmap in Chapter 7 should address what we want them to feel, think and do when they arrive at our website, landing pages, web based applications, mobile apps or on your companies social profiles.

We're going to want to have paid advertising that finds our ideal customers on a social platform of some sort, for example Facebook, Instagram, Twitter or LinkedIn.

Once we've identified ideal customers and they've opted in for something, or perhaps there is a place for cold email marketing. But either way, we need systems in place so that we can automate every digital marketing channel. Web, Social, Mobile, Email.

"Systematize the predictable, and humanize everything else."
- Isadore Sharp, founder of Four Seasons Hotels

How To Decide What to Automate, What To Focus On for Growth

I was listening to an episode of the 10X Podcast by marketing expert Joe Polish and Dan Sullivan, the co-founder of the Strategic Coach program.

Joe Polish's marketing expertise has been utilized to build thousands of businesses and has generated hundreds of millions of dollars for both large corporations and small family-owned businesses.

Dan Sullivan is the author of over 30 publications, a visionary, innovator, and gifted conceptual thinker. Dan has over 35 years' experience as a highly regarded speaker, consultant, strategic planner, and coach to entrepreneurial individuals and groups.

In the episode of the 10X podcast titled "How To Change Your Game", Dan Sullivan outlined what I think is a super-effective 90 day planning system. After learning this system I quickly realized that it helps cut through a lot of confusion about 'what to automate' while also helping focus your personal entrepreneurial efforts on High Value activities.

Dan suggests that entrepreneurs come up with three lists labelled A,B and C.

The A List is a list of three things in your business that _irritate you_. That is the first list and he gives his personal example of things in business that might irritate you. People, situations, activities or tasks and obligations.

The **B List** is of of three items that are the things in your business that are "OK". They're going well, they result in cash flow.

The final list is the **C List.** This is the list of _three things in your business that fascinate you_. These are the three most exciting and inspiring parts of your business right now. Then he drew the following 3 circles to illustrate these lists. And he draws this out as follows:

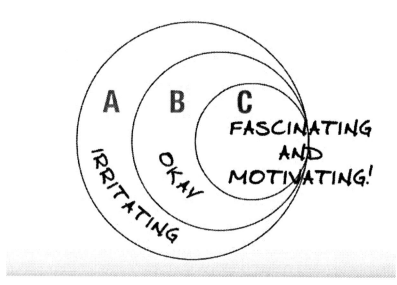

He goes on to suggest that this exercise be conducted once every 90 days. The for the next 90 days the focus is to **eliminate the things on your A-List**. The parts of your business that irritate you.

Then you **systematize and automate** the things on your B-List. This is how you continually automate your business. By following this planning process, continual automation becomes part of your business DNA.

Finally, your C-List is what can have huge impact on your business. This is where you can achieve great growth and so it's very inspiring. This is most likely the list that will generate the Growth for your business. Here's how this might look.

At the bottom of the chart above take a look at the 'Game Changers'. These are the three things in each of the A,B,C categories that will majorly impact your business with positive growth. These are the three things that we want to create a scorecard for and a digital platform

Non Strategic days/hours	New Digital Products days/hours	Strategic Initiatives days/hours
10% 0%	20% 10%	70% 90%
All Clients Inside Scorecards	All Concepts Geared Towards 10X	Affiliate Partnership Meetings
Reports and Dashboards on Key Metrics	Focus and Project Managers	Podcast Guests
3 Important Things/ Day	Mobile App Project	Content Creation and Speaking

Making educated, data-driven decisions

Management thinker Peter Drucker is often famously quoted as saying that "you can't manage what you can't measure." So in other words we create a way to measure three impactful things per quarter and we digitize this. We find a way to collect the data on these three items and report on them.

When we identify what 'success' means in our business, we can create metrics that give us feedback on how we are progressing towards that definition.

103

Once we have a list of irritating things that need to be automated- these are important but most likely repetitive or mundane tasks - we have also used the B and C lists to define our business' success criteria. Then we create processes and use some form of software application to automate that process. Eliminate the variability of human choice or behavior.

Then we are free to focus upon high value activities that will move the business forward towards growth.

Clarifying expectations for team members, continually redefining success criteria, and then measuring against that criteria are the right steps to creating winning systems and automated workflows in our business.

Chapter Summary Points

1. Crafting an Automate and Grow Strategic Plan is a crucial first step
2. This will help you articulate the benefits of implementing new business systems and approaches
3. Ideally Automate & Grow becomes a cultural approach for your entire organization
4. Applying Dan Sullivan's A,B,C approach is an effective way for entrepreneurs to continually find new automations and focus on growth activities for their businesses.

References

http://www.smartinsights.com/goal-setting-evaluation/vision-setting/vision-mission-statements-for-ecommerce-and-digital-marketing/

https://blog.hubspot.com/marketing/inspiring-company-mission-statements

https://www.accenture.com/us-en/blogs/blogs-digital-what-is-digital-strategy

https://www.projecttimes.com/articles/10-steps-to-creating-a-project-plan.html

https://www.growthinstitute.com/mbc/scaling-up/

http://10xtalk.com/changing-your-game-with-dan-sullivan/

https://www.youtube.com/watch?v=ru_fcQFiMak

https://hbr.org/2017/07/6-digital-strategies-and-why-some-work-better-than-others

https://www.accenture.com/us-en/blogs/blogs-digital-high-performance-delivered

http://mspmentor.net/managed-services/102214/10-tips-master-art-innovation

https://www.facebook.com/WiseGuywithGuyKawasaki/videos/1458453017577443/

https://guykawasaki.com/the-art-of-evangelism/

Chapter 5: Marketing Automation

Much of what we have talked about to this point has been around automation of processes. What about growth?

I think inside of the marketing team of your company lies two key areas of growth. One is Product Marketing. The other is Digital Marketing and its automation.

For a moment, let's assume we have a great, differentiated product.

All things being equal, if you have a good to great product and just need more of the right type of customers, then the use of Marketing Automation will be key to your growth. This is how we generate leads, stay in touch with prospects and advance visitors through their buying journey on your platform. In the end, that's the reason to invest in marketing automation and to have a plan and resources invested in this area of your business.

Growth Hacking

Growth hacking is the marketing approach that involves a process of rapid experimentation across marketing channels. It can also be used hand in hand with rapid product iterations and product development to test potential customer feedback. Using the experiments and data as feedback, this new breed of marketer finds product and market combinations that they can scale up once 'unlocked'.

I won't lie, I am no growth hacker. The trial and error and reading of the tea leaves doesn't fit my personality. However, we can learn from the approach by deploying technology, tools and, maybe most importantly, the right people resources to grow our own businesses. I cannot emphasize this enough, the person or people behind this effort will be super important.

A growth hacking marketer will implement a process where they identify a list or target client, testing ad and email copy using email marketing, SEO and content (among others) with the intent of finding a pattern. Then, once identified, they are basically exploiting that pattern, ratcheting it up for volume and higher rates of conversion.

> A growth hacker is not a replacement for a marketer. A growth hacker is not better than a marketer. A growth hacker is just different than a marketer. To use the most succinct definition from Sean's post, "A growth hacker is a person whose true north is growth."
> Source:
> https://www.quicksprout.com/the-definitive-guide-to-growth-hacking/

What is Marketing Automation?

Marketing Automation is the use of software tools that allow a marketer to increase the number of potential touches to potential customers. It scales out the targeting, attraction, identification and activation of Ideal Clients.

Marketing automation platforms can contain a mix of features, but mainly they revolve around email marketing. Core functions of many marketing automation platforms revolve around building campaigns, adding contacts or prospects to campaigns. The automated part is where a series of sequential messages are built using rules. There are measurements of when an email is sent to a prospect, if they opened the email (read it), forwarded the email, replied to it. Rules typically are triggered by time or these events.

For example, you can usually send an email spaced out by days, day 1, day 3 day 7 and so on. You can also build rules that fire off different versions of a staged message.

Beyond email marketing, marketing automation can also address other digital marketing channels or offer features around email marketing. This may or may not include tools to build landing pages, opt in forms for websites, social media posting, pay per click campaigns, organic content marketing - search engine optimization (SEO for short).

"In a nutshell, marketing automation refers to software that automates your marketing for you. The software is designed to help you prioritize and execute your marketing tasks in a more streamlined and efficient way."

Source: What is Marketing Automation: A Beginners Guide. Hubspot

What Does Marketing Automation Allow You to Accomplish?

The whole point of marketing automation is to attract enough Leads into your business that are far enough along in their buying journey that they convert into a realistic propect when handed over to Sales. Or they decide to buy when they interact with your online ecommerce platform.

This allows your business to scale and grow. It also allows marketers in your business to, over time (hopefully), use information to reduce the cost per customer closer towards zero. It also allows you to re-market to your existing customers and capture additional dollars from those who have already bought from you.

Marketing automation software can also aid in the post-sales support of customers. All with little to no human interaction.

Human interactions, such as the type typically needed in customer-facing conversations for Sales or Support, can be slow and expensive, especially if you have a low margin or low-ticket item service or product.

Examples of Marketing Automation Features

Most marketing automation software centers around a few potential key features.

1. Email marketing
2. Web marketing
3. Paid online advertising
4. Organic web content marketing
5. Social marketing
6. Mobile marketing

Our focus in Automating our Marketing Plan is to achieve a number of key actions in our business with minimum human actions day to day. We want to use technology to put these programs into play:

1. Lead Generation

2. Lead Management
3. Blogging and Social Media
4. Search Optimization
5. Marketing Analytics
6. Email and Automation

Types of Marketing to Consider Automating

When talking about the different types of marketing automation applications, we'd first want to talk about the different types of marketing you're going to engage in, and then we can look for technology to support this. There's really six that we'll focus on here. The first is email marketing, we'll talk about web marketing, paid online advertising, content marketing, social marketing, and mobile marketing. For email marketing, I would say there's three types of email marketing that you're going to want to engage in, and the type of platform that you choose will vary a little bit for each of them, cold email, opt in, and then nurturing. Let me explain what the difference between these are in my mind.

Cold email campaigns, you're probably not going to be able to use all marketing automation or email marketing tools to conduct cold email campaigns. Many platforms require you have an opted in list, whereas for cold campaigns, there's only certain platforms that will accept a non-opt in list.

For example, cold email campaigns would be by some people considered the bad type of email marketing, which is spam, or is it? This has become an alternative really to cold calling or in conjunction with cold calling where a sales development rep is trying to make contact with a prospective client.

This is really not mass emailing. What this is is an SDR has a list that they've build of specific accounts and contacts at those accounts, or they're trying to discover contacts.

Typically, it's a modest outreach of 50 to 100 contacts a day. There's still automation once they're put into a campaign, but the types of messages are very different. Not to get into too much detail, but essentially these are touchpoint type messages. Sent over a number of days.

The day one message might be an intro message. Day three is a followup on the intro message. Day five would be a followup with some sort of a case study. Day seven would be a touchpoint to find out who the right contact is.

You're just really trying to prompt the potential contact to identify whether they fit into your category of business and if they're the right person to be talking to. Essentially these are staged within a sequence of emails that are in the email marketing platform over a series of days.

The the Sales Development Rep (SDR) might also be calling that specific individual to try and get them live. In the end, they're trying to either arrange a meeting or gather information, discover the correct contacts at the account.

This can be also useful in combination with **LinkedIn Marketing** where you might have a contact, you add them at the account, you add them to a cold email sequence but it's warmed up a little because you've also requested them on LinkedIn, and you're trying to reach out to them, call them just to discover where they're at, if they're the right contact, and if they're engaged in any sort of buying process.

You can move them to a nurturing campaign or opt in if they aren't in a meeting buying cycle and they haven't told you to stop emailing them (See below). There's a bunch of legal rules around doing cold email that make it so it's not spam. (CanSpam) Again, Cold Email is not mass emailing tens or thousands of contacts. It's really outreach to specific contacts and then giving them the option to pull out of your campaign.

Opt in email, typically is where the receiver agrees to receive information from you. Often we're using a lead magnet of some sort like a free giveaway in exchange for that person's opt in. It might be a free ebook, it might be an infographic, it might be a webinar. We're really sending, again, a series of emails in this scenario over a couple days.

You're creating a campaign where they're getting a sequence of emails. At the end of it, ideally what you're trying to do is give them a specific offer or action. The offer might be a specific purchase that they can make online. Now we're getting into sales automation with an e-commerce purchase, or it might be trying to get them to set up an appointment, or some other action that fits with your sales cycle and their buying journey.

Nurturing emails campaigns, are distinguished from cold email campaigns by the fact that these are more long-term, stay-in-touch type campaigns.

An email automation platform is going to be more forgiving for opt in and for nurturing campaigns because these tend to be opted-in contacts. These campaigns tend to be sequential emails over a different period of time and with a different message and purpose.

Emails are sent over months, not days. The idea is that these contacts fit an Ideal Customer profile but are not far enough along in their buying journey for us to engage in our Sales Process. They are most like only at Stage 1 or 2 of their typical buying journey:

1. ***Customer has recognized there is a problem***
2. ***When they are researching solutions to that problem***
3. When they are selecting a solution
4. When they have bought your solution

The goal of Nurture Campaigns is to make sure that you're not losing touch with this contact and company until they're ready to put their hand back out and indicate that they're ready to select a solution or buy.

This might be just an attempt to generate an opt in back to a shorter sequence where you're trying to identify when that contact is ready to engage in their buying journey again, and it's appropriate to try and warm them up and get them ready for a sales process.

"As a marketer, your most valuable asset is your marketing database. But your database is only as powerful as you make it. You've put a lot of work into attracting leads. However, research from Gleanster suggests that, even when it comes to qualified leads, more than 50% of leads aren't ready to buy on the day they first convert on your site. If you call up these leads and push them into making a decision right away, you will likely lose them."

Source: How to Master Marketing Automation Going Beyond Email. The Advanced Guide to Optimizing Your Marketing Funnel with Lead Nurturing by Hubspot

Web Marketing is a broad category, and there's going to be different tools, depending on what you need. For example, this might be search engine optimization, could be also search engine marketing. You're trying to create articles and content typically for your website, possibly for social platforms. You're going to want to optimize this so that it's picked up by organic search terms or you're targeting particular traffic using search engine marketing methods.

When you're looking at some sort of marketing automation, you're going to want to create publishing schedules. You might want to have syndication. You're going to be using mostly your website or social platforms to get traffic back to your website. There's going to be specific tools and platforms that are focused around **SEO** or **SEM** to help you do this.

Search Engine Optimization

Moz is a leading search engine optimization agency that also provides excellent SEO application tools. I usually recommend someone not familiar with SEO concepts to start with their 101 guide to SEO. When reading through this, you may quickly do as I do: recognize that you're not an expert in this and need a team resource and tools that is.

You can check out their guide here: https://moz.com/learn/seo. The conclusion I quickly come to is the following:

- Your website needs to be Search Engine Optimized
- This can seem like voodoo to me but in the end if you have the right approach it makes sure that you receive organic traffic
- Once your website is set up correctly so that search engines can index it, there is little substitution for producing good content on an ongoing basis
- This can provide focused traffic from Ideal Clients
- You should not ignore how to convert organic traffic
- There are ways to gather details on anonymous visitors to make them opted-in visitors
- This needs to become your goal if you're to capitalize upon this traffic or you will see little return on your investment and you will become frustrated, or at least that is my personal experience

Search Engine Marketing

This is paid marketing that generates traffic from search engines using PPC (Pay Per Click) or other display advertising. The value here is of course you can target Ideal Clients using key words and put ads into optimized spacing by outbidding competitors.

This can be a source of traffic, but often is expensive. Using paid advertising can bring anonymous visitors to your websites and landing pages. It is therefore critical in order to get the right return on investment that you gain opt-in where anonymous visitors come to your digital properties and identify themselves. So you need a part of your traffic and conversion plan that gets 'opt in'. You need to lure the visitor in with a lead magnet or video or other tactics to turn them into an identified visitor.

I would suggest that unless you are an expert in this area that you need a team resource that is focused upon optimizing not only the traffic but the conversion of that traffic. They also will either come armed or need to be armed with certain digital tools.

Search Engine Land is an online marketing blog that provide articles, ideas and tools around web marketing and I recommend reading their explanation on SEM. SOURCE: What Is Paid Search? SearchEngineLand. You should understand the tenants of SEM I think and be engaged in the creation of a strategy around paid marketing.

The most important thing whether you hire an outside consultant (I think so) or service provider (another good option) to manage this or if you deem this important enough to hire a full time employee. This depends on how big you are and the level of focus and management you can provide inside your company. The bottom line is that you need to trust whoever is leading your SEM and SEO efforts and you will need to agree on the definition of success for SEM and SEO efforts.

Clear expectations and a way to measure their their activity through reports and touch base meetings will be critical. I have gone in on this type of team resource half hearted and it dooms the effort to fail if you don't have good communication, understanding of their tactics and plan and clear expectations of what you want out of paid search campaigns.

You can blow your brains out on budgets sometimes and if you don't get the results you want (for me this is about conversion on dollars spent into dollars earned) you're going to be dumping buckets of money down an abyss. Rather than being happy you will be distracted by the black hole of money this can become.

When you're evaluating a marketing automation platform, SEO may or may not be a big component of the technology you're trying to evaluate and deciding to buy. There are specific tools that can be used for keyword research, can be used of publishing, can be used of syndication of content and analytics. These might be separate from your marketing automation platform or in some cases they might be a part of this software.

Local online marketing may be applicable to your business, so you might be targeting local keywords. There are tools to help you publish and target content based upon that focus. Over time this tends to be a little bit slower type of traffic and conversion, so you want to use tools that are going to help you stay consistent and can be published over time.

For **SEM paid online advertising**, this is where you're buying pay per click ads or display ads. For each of those scenarios, you're going to want to have a couple things in your marketing automation platform.

One feature will be some form of web analytics. This is software like Google Analytics to track web visits to your web page and landing pages. You may even have third party web analytics capabilities inside of your marketing automation platform. At the very

117

least you pay be able to connect your Google Analytics account to your marketing automation platform to report on web traffic and patterns.

A lot of times you'll want landing page capabilities built in to your marketing automation platform.

For example, Pardot is an email marketing platform that is part of the Salesforce Marketing Cloud suite. Pardot allows marketers to create landing pages and opt in form code. These can be connected with Google Analytics so that you can track the visitors arriving at your landing page, how long they were 'on' the page, what they did on the page (click, leave etc). These are capabilities that you're going to want to evaluate in your marketing automation platform and this will be an important tool for tracking visitor behavior.

When you create and promote lead magnets like reports, free ebooks, infographics, videos etc. you're also going to want a way inside of your marketing automation platform to manage the content (store and forward) and to track the results, the conversions.

Then you want to be able to grab-opt in from visitors . In the end, this information has to end up somewhere. It either ends up in your marketing automation platform in the form of contact records or in CRM as new Lead records.

Content marketing. Content comes in many forms. For B2B customers often you're creating lead magnets. You might also have a blog or vlog. This might involve your video YouTube channel or Vimeo. You may want to start publishing podcasts as well as having social tie in to this content. You're going to want to evaluate if you need a marketing automation platform for publishing, syndicating, promoting this type of content.

Social marketing, this might be where you're commenting on content that's related to your business. A good example of this is that often Reddit or Quora are sites where there's business-related topics or consumer-related topics that might relate to your product, and you can go through the process of using a platform to identify threads using keywords.

There are social marketing platforms that will allow you to do this and then to publish responses, commenting and then linking back to landing pages or pages on your website to generate traffic that's relevant. For example Hootsuite, falcon.io or SEMRush might be examples of applications that provide you tools to manage social posts and marketing.

Social marketing could also be just your direct regular publishing activity around Facebook, Twitter, Instagram, LinkedIn, and even YouTube, and trying to generate traffic, either subscribers and followers or just traffic back to your content and offers. Usually though if you are publishing to multiple social profiles and platforms any of the above sort of applications would be very beneficial.

Some of the Application Names You May Recognize

Examples of marketing automation platforms you might recognize are HubSpot, Marketo, Infusionsoft, Salesforce Pardot, Reply.io, Mailchimp, Constant Contact... just to name a few. Each of these platforms has specific features and a specific target audience. Before you decide on which application or combination of applications is right for you, we need a game plan.

Traffic and Conversion Plan

Your traffic and conversion plan is the tactical real world written game plan that will guide marketing automation and, frankly, all marketing efforts.

There are 7 sections you need to complete your traffic and conversion plan

1. Mission - Your Story of Why
2. Ideal Client & Client Personae
3. Buying Journey
4. Sales Process
5. Traffic Sources
6. Lead Capture and Activation
7. Conversion (going from suspect to lead to opportunity)

Competition is For Losers

Peter Thiel the co-founder of PayPal, venture capitalist (famed for investing the first $500,000 in Facebook) and author of *Zero to One,* clearly states that Capitalism and Competition are at odds. This is because in Economics, perfect competition sees the consumer winning to the extent that all profits go to zero.

Rather than only defining your success as a business based upon profit or retained earnings, Thiel suggests that you want to create a monopoly. Not in the classic sense of an immoral corporate giant crushing competitors. Instead, he suggests that great companies do something so well that others cannot compete with them.

Thiel further articulates that this means focusing upon a 'great product or service' that is unique. Those companies in your chosen sector of the marketplace that are uniquely addressing a problem in a way other businesses do not or cannot, capture the most value. This does not mean they are of course generating the most top line revenue.

Thiel also uses a great example comparing the economic value in 2012 retained by Google vs the Airline Industry. He shows how Google keeps more in retained earnings than the Airlines which are largely homogenous and undifferentiated. Goole by contrast is a very unique organization that delivers great value and thus has a position akin to Thiel's definition of a monopoly business.

Thus, despite top line revenue produced by Airlines that is triple that of Google, Google keeps 33 cents of every dollar generated. The airlines, they on the otherhand produce net losses.

Check out Thiel's famed Stanford University Center for Professional Development Talk on the subject. https://www.youtube.com/watch?v=bVV26yRjwq0. I think this is a world class education on how we can all position our businesses for growth. I don't know of a better model.

Let's just note, that I put this here under the Marketing portion of Automate + Grow because while this work is in my opinion a strategic obligation of business leaders, it falls to marketing to express this unique market positioning. So, before we start automating any outreach to generate leads, we really need to nail down what we are as a business to the world.

If the leaders of a business will not take this step, then it falls to marketing leaders to at least try to define this to some extent or another through two primary marketing functions: Communication and Product.

It is also possible that Product development including the product's unique features and capabilities falls to some other group in your business. You still will rely upon marketing to tell this story of the unique features and positioning of the company's products over and over to attract clients to our business.

Your Story of Why

We discussed before the need to emotionally connect with buyers. Most companies have some sort of statement—written or otherwise—that positions them in the market. This starts with What They Do. What product or service do they build, sell to customers? This starts the process of focusing your marketing efforts, because it leads to the inevitable question of "Ok, great, who will buy this?"

In his book *Start with Why* and his related TED Talk on the same topic, Simon Sinek outlined how employees and customers will connect with a business emotionally. He describes in both the clearest & simplest approach to distinguishing your business in a competitive world.

You can check out Simon's TED Talk here: https://www.youtube.com/watch?v=IPYeCltXpxw

Sinek points out that every organization knows WHAT they do, generally. Usually some even can express HOW they do this thing they do. That is, most businesses have a unique selling position around their product or service. This is the **How** of their business.

How they are unique and How they deliver a unique product or service.

This comes down to the features and capabilities of your company's product or service offering.

Great, this is important. However, in this day and age when customers research 80% of their purchases online before they make a selection, this features list becomes fodder for the discerning buyer. They can make choices based upon comparable features without much influence or connection to your purpose.

That information can sometimes be confusing rather than convincing, and sometimes buyers online make a choice in a bubble without human interaction and with incomplete information, or with poorly communicated information. The quality of your online presentation of How and What you do will be important. However, nothing will be as important as the story of **Why** you do What you do or as the reasoning behind How you Do it.

The **Story of Why** presents your vision of the world and the problem(s) that exist. It presents to your Ideal Client a mission of your business to solve this problem by providing a unique offering.

This is critical to gain the attention of the Ideal Client. You can have all the marketing automation in the world that money can buy. If you do not grab their attention, do not explain your cause, your mission it is going to be more difficult to get them to identify themselves by opt in or other means, you're toast. You can do it; you can bribe them, offer them free stuff, ideas and content. You, however, can really motivate your Ideal Clients by clearly communicating the "Why" behind the What and How of your business.

Before you drop a dime on technology around marketing, you must at least know your story of 'What' and 'How' you do what you do.

To truly orient your business towards growth, however, I think first understanding and then telling your story of Why will properly position you in a noisy world.

Then, automating the process of telling this story and all its supporting materials becomes much, much easier.

Check out his book and chapter three on the "Golden Circle." This is where Simon articulates this theory that explains the power of this Story of Why vs just 'How' and 'What.'
Source: Start With Why, Simon Sinek

Ideal Client Profile

Who is your Ideal Client? This is important. Online marketing and traffic can give you amazing tools to target customers in Business to Business (B2B) or Business to Consumer (B2C) channels. The more detailed information you have on your customer, the more specific you can get when driving traffic.

- B2B or B2C
- Geography or Location
- Age
- Sex
- Interests
- Income/Revenues
- Business Size
- Industry

Buyer Persona or Customer Avatars

Once you begin to quantify your Ideal Client, you will need to create a profile of them. Each Buyer profile (or persona) will form the foundation of each of your campaigns. It will tell you who they are very clearly; the problems they have; how you solve these problems. Then, your task as a marketer is to understand what they are looking for (solutions, asking questions) and where they are doing this (Google, YouTube, LinkedIn etc.).

The more you do to create your customer avatars (profiles) the more specific you can be on the digital marketing channels you use to target those ideal customers. You will also want to define the reasons those idea customers will connect with your 'Story of Why' This will serve as the foundation for your content, email, and display campaigns.

Buying Journey

One you have profiled who your Ideal Customer is using Personas or a Customer Avatar for each, you can begin to understand the process they go through to making a purchase. Imagine and document the questions they ask along their buying journey. Quantify and details the information they look for to solve their problem. At what point are they typically ready to buy what process have they gone through, t questions have the answered - and why? Detail the critical factors that leads them to make a final buying decision between various options and alternatives.

125

There are 4 stages a buyer goes through in their journey that you will want to document, explore and understand.

- Recognition of a Problem
- Search for a Solution
- Search for Options
- Selection of Alternatives

Sales Process

Once you understand the journey your buyer goes through, you can start to tailor an experience for this Ideal Client. This is, roughly, your Sales Process. There are 6 stages, generally, to your Sales process

- Prospecting or Lead Generation
- Qualification
- Presentation
- Quotation or Product Configuration
- Negotiation
- Object Handling
- Closing the Sale or Transaction

Depending on the dollar value, complexity, and ease of buying your product, the time from stage 1 to 7 of your Sales Process will vary. You will want to identify in each of these the key steps in the sales process.

I described this as an experience because old fashioned Sales Processes are clunky and too transparent. Instead you want to think in terms of how you lead a customer in a positive manner to solve their problem using content. How you meet their expectations while researching that gives them the confidence your solution to their problem is the best.

Marketing's job and how they employ marketing automation is to provide the potential buyer with an experience of emotional connection that plants the seeds for either a final e-commerce transaction or a direct one to one human interaction with a Sales person.

Traffic Sources

Where do your Ideal Clients hang out? How will you find them, attract them and get them to click on your ad, email or post? Sources for example are:

Category	Examples of Source	Examples of Tools	Notes
Email, Cold	InsideView, infoFree, InfoUSA, Dunn and Bradstreet, Data.com etc.	Reply.io, MailChimp, HonchoMail, Infusionsoft	You buy a list of cold contacts, either individuals or at companies, that you think match your Ideal Client profile. You load these up into an appropriate marketing automation tool. You create cold outreach and try to warm the list up through their opt in.
Email, Opted In	You have an opted in List	Reply.io, Pardot, Constant Contact, ActiveDemand, Infusionsoft	You have a list of opted-in subscribers who liked something you offered or did enough to sign up and agree to hear from you again by email. You create automated messaging and conversion points to help potential buyers actively engaged in a Buying journey to advance this journey, preferably towards your offering.
Organic Web Traffic	Someone comes to your website	Content Management System like WordPress, tools from HubSpot, Pardot or Infusionsoft like web to lead forms, web tracking code	You publish articles. Hopefully, search engines rank your content on topics and you get traffic because someone clicks on your article link. Someone shows up on your website, anonymously searches around & reads. Platforms like Pardot, Infusionsoft and HubSpot can help you compile information on anonymous visitors, like what pages and content they are consuming.

Paid Search Advertising	Display or text ads on Search engine	Google AdWords	Since it can be very challenging to rank for keywords in search engines, you can always just buy display ads for your content or conversion pages and pay per click through.
Social Platform	Build a following on your social profile and post content	Facebook Instagram LinkedIn Twitter SnapChat YouTube	You have subscribers or followers and they respond to your posted content.
Social Paid Display Advertising	Display ad on Social network	Facebook Ads Twitter Ads YouTube Instagram Ads LinkedIn Advertising	You can pay for promoted posts and display ads targeted to segmented users on platforms like Instagram. You can have inline display ads or promoted posts, shout outs from influencer networks or profiles.

Lead Capture and Activation

This is the process of taking an anonymous visitor or prospect and getting them to identify themselves. They opt in or request information and you capture an email or mobile contact, maybe their name.

Conversion

Get prospects to:
- buy
- ask for more information
- ask for help buying

You go from an identified prospect to an interested one. Someone says they need pricing, product configuration or they simply buy on the spot.

You have a traffic and conversion plan, now what?

OK, you have a game plan. Now what? First you can see what capabilities you need. Do you need cold email marketing or just email automation for warm campaigns? Do you want to track and profile anonymous web visitors? Will you need a social posting application?

What is the state of your website?

Visually, functionally, is it integrated to a back-end database or customer portal? Does it talk to your CRM? What is your CRM? Do you know what CRM is?

Start a Campaign

Time to start testing your plan. This is where you need someone patient and responsive enough to build an automated campaign and to adjust it to implement your traffic conversion plan piece by piece.

When is the right time to start this?

Now! Start with a hypothesis, create a campaign and start driving traffic. Monitor the opt ins, clicks, the replies.

Start small, measure results. Scale it up.

Content Creation

The process of Content Creation can be arduous. Some content types are easier to create than others but you will need and want a steady stream of the stuff to keep followers on social media engaged, grab the interest of potential customers, get them to identify themselves, or to help your buyer progress through their buying journey from one stage to another.

The type of content obviously depends upon the type of buyer you have (B2C, B2B) and the complexity of their buying journey. Increasingly, however, the quality of presentation lends itself to more casual conversational content. Marketing jargon heavy content is again more obvious and less human.

Buyers are increasingly skeptical of old school jargon heavy content. In a world of reality-based content, the lines are blurred between educational and entertainment. Even if you're selling a piece of software, the more relatable and human your content is the better.

Unprofessional? Well, let's say you might be able to convey that you're professional, but if you don't connect personally or emotionally you're in trouble.

Are you an expert? Does your software have a magical solution? Are you cooler or more reliable than the competition? In any case, you have to decide on the visual messaging (look & feel) of your content and what purpose each piece has in advancing the buying journey.

Or you can just pump out volume. Apply the 'All attention is good attention' theory.

Whatever the case, decide ahead of time. Decide how and who will produce content. Who approves it? How often do you publish? How will you drive traffic to content? What is the conversion? What action do you want the reader to take?

Start producing the content and then publishing it.

Here are some examples of content marketers will create:

- Blog posts
- Guest blog posts
- Social posts
- Videos
- Checklists
- Ebooks
- Webinars
- Reports
- Memes
- Images
- Infographics
- Podcast

The types of content that you should be producing are as follows:

Number one with a bullet is you need to be producing some form of regular **blog posts**. This is where you're writing articles on your own website relevant to your customers, so you need to think in terms of what are the typical problems my customer has? What are the solutions that my service, product or software offers to those problems?

Then, break it down into articles. You also want to look at it from a search engine point of view: what terms are your ideal clients searching for on search engines and how would they potentially find my article? You want to write quality content here, so think in terms of problems and solutions that your product, service, or software offers, and the benefits to the customer. Offer real information provided by experts in the form of a blog post.

Guest blog posts. This is where you're writing topical articles for the blogs of other industry experts, industry-specific websites, complimentary service providers. Anywhere your ideal client might hang out and conduct research. As a guest blogger you are able to establish your expertise and attract interest potentially in your products, services or software.

So, for example, if I were writing on the topic of search engine optimization, I would approach Searchland.com and try to offer them a blog on a particular topic that they publish blog posts on. If I was writing on the topic of CRM I might be a guest blogger on CRMLeaders.org

Social posts. This is the content you post to your various social media accounts like Facebook, Twitter, and LinkedIn. The idea of course is to write content on your area of expertise that will attract potential prospects. You can now boost these posts by paying to promote posts on Facebook or Twitter to a particular target audience. This can be an effective way to grow your followers and find prospects. This is an evolving space and like other content strategies listed here, you're going to want someone on your team that understands and adapts to trends while effectively managing your profiles.

Video is a powerful tool. Video content has taken over Internet traffic. "Globally, IP video traffic will be 82 percent of all consumer Internet traffic by 2021, up from 73 percent in 2016" according to CISCO Networks' Visual Networking Index: Forecast and Methodology, 2016–2021 Creating video content is probably the single most important content type today as a result.

Publishing video content to your website, syndicating video through your social profiles for traffic and of course publishing to YouTube are all awesome tools to attract, educate and support buyers both pre and post sale.

YouTube on its own is a very powerful search engine. It's obviously tied in to (owned by) Google, so that people searching for answers to questions may specifically search for video responses. Buyers may not use Google to search but they may search directly on YouTube itself. YouTube is now the second-used search engine in the world next to Google.

Vimeo is another effective platform where you would create videos similar to blog content. You can create videos on particular topics that answer questions.

Checklists. Producing content checklists are a must. These can be very effective lead magnets. Checklists are very effective because they basically give you the reader the best answers around a problem or idea. They're easily consumed, and in world of information overload, they can simplify solutions and answers to pressing problems in a very quick and clear manner.

Ebooks and books. Whether you're writing a book and publishing it printed on your own, either self-publishing it or through a publisher, eBooks and books can be effective types of content to communicate key ideas.

Being the author of a book communicates that you're an expert in your field.

Most software companies will publish books to frame the philosophy and practice behind the software applications they sell. An example of this is   Mark

Roberge with his book 'The Sales Acceleration Formula.'

Mark is a co-founder of Hubspot, which is a very successful marketing automation platform. Mark lays out the philosophy of how to establish an effective marketing automation program in your business one that marries sales and marketing functions.

Webinars can be an incredibly effective way to build an audience, get opt-in for a particular date and time, communicate an idea that solves a problem, and then even at the end of it, make a digital product or consulting offer. These are a powerful form of content that can lead directly to generating new leads and sales opportunities.

They're usually live but can also be used are replays once recorded for future opt in and playback. Webinars tend to be very interactive, and give you the opportunity to have communication on a mass scale with potential buyers or prospects or customers. Then again, you want to think in terms of conversion of your webinars to something, whether they get something for free or they buy something that's a special offer that's part of the webinar.

Reports. Reports on a particular subject are effective content piece. This can relate to the software, services or products that you're suggesting they buy from you. A report that is industry-specific, addresses a problem or a need of your client can be a very effective tool to attract buyers and to gain opt in as lead magnets.

Based upon the topic of the report, you can understand if whether or not if this person's interested in this particular topic, are they a prospect for my product, service or software and where they might be at in their current buying journey.

Memes. Memes are the use of a picture with overlaying text, and they can be an idea or concept. These can be effective in both B2B- and B2C-type scenarios. Typically, memes are going to be posted on social networks.

Instagram is a really good example where meme content can be effective in quickly communicating an idea. You could use humor. You can make pointed statements. Your shared meme can be problem-based,. This is an easy way to communicate an idea that whoever the viewer is can quickly relate to, and then you can come up with a way that you gain a follower, you gain a conversion from that meme content. If it's something the follower likes, they will also share it to echo the idea you share in the meme.

Images, similarly, can be used and syndicated where you can share images on social networks and based upon the images, they may have text as part of them, which I guess probably relates them back to a meme. But maybe it's an image that's .

Infographics. Infographics can communicate facts or a story with images and text. This is an effective content piece that provide a visual representation of ideas, research, facts. Infographics can also be a call-to-action. When used as a lead magnet visitors provide email contact details in exchange for receiving a copy of the infographic. Infographics can also be shared on social networks.

135

Podcasts and guest podcasting. Podcasts are all the rage. By 2017 one hundred and twelve million Americans have listened to a podcast. That number is up 11 percent from 2016. Overall, 40 percent of Americans age 12 or older have listened to a podcast at some point. With the massive rise in popularity of podcasts and now podcast video content comes and incredible opportunity. In the past you would have to spend money on television advertisements. TV stations and channels controlled what programming was on air to attract their audience. Now, you can simply create content that is relevant to your business audience and grow your listener base through promotion. You can also find podcasters in your business ecosystem and offer them another terrific podcast guest with exciting ideas and content. By producing your own interview show or guesting on show you have an incredible forum to discuss your customers' problems that you solve.

Source: The 11 Critical Podcast Statistics of 2017, Edison Research http://sumo.ly/x9Hb
http://www.convinceandconvert.com/podcast-research/the-11-critical-podcast-statistics-of-2017/

Conversion Tools

So now that we've produced content, we may want to get opt-in where we're taking an anonymous visitor and we're getting them to identify themselves in exchange for some sort of content. So here's some typical conversion tools that may be in your marketing automation platforms, or you might buy as a one-off or built.

- Opt in Forms
- Autoresponders
- Live Chat
- Web to Lead

- Free Trials
- Customer Registration
- Subscription to Social
- Single Sign On
- Social Follow

Opt-in forms. This can be as simple as a web form that you put on your website. It can also be a feature in your marketing automation platform, where it will generate opt-in forms and you can gather information that will go directly into your CRM or into your marketing automation platform.

Autoresponders. When someone does opt-in, maybe you want them to receive a notification by email thanking them for their opting-in and delivering content, so Autoresponders can be a feature of your marketing automation. They can also just be a feature where you're creating an email address on your email server, and it includes a body of a message in the Autoresponder email.

Live chat. This can be an interesting conversion tool for websites or landing pages, where you can add something like tawk.to or other live messengers. If someone comes to your website, they're a visitor, and it pops up a chat window that says, "Hi. Can I help you?" This can be effective for your website or even landing pages.

Web to Lead. This is where you could create an opt-in or an inquiry form on your website. You convert that person into a known factor where they include their name, email, and a question or a problem they want a response back to. This can show up in CRM, for example, as a lead, and then you can create lead cues to assign it to a sales or support person to respond.

Free Trials and Demos. If you a digital software application or mobile app software you may want to give the customer an opportunity to try your SaaS application. Perhaps you offer a demonstration of your product or service to prove its value. This can be an effective way to gain conversion on your website visits. Pitch the value of the application, product or service then give immediate access to it.

The act of registering for your free trial or demo, converts anonymous visitors into known users.

Another useful tool can be a live demonstration of your product over the web. Again this might be a recorded demo, a simulated demo or a webinar walk through of your product or software.

Then maybe the free trial expires or there's an offer in the free trial to convert to a paying customer. Another idea is to offer a Freemium version of your application, product or service. A useful but not fully featured version that a single customer can use. For example if you sign up for Zapier, Wufoo or Mailchimp there are free versions of these SaaS applications. once you outgrow them and need or features, storage then you can upgrade to a full paid version.

Customer registration. So maybe you allow them to register on your website or application or for free access to a customer area. This where the user then provides their name, email, etc. and are automatically added to your email list.

This is effective because you're converting an anonymous person into a known prospect and they are either activating as a customer or prospect through the steps of registration.

Even if you don't offer software, what if you offer a free customer portal? Offer a free content area of your website that contains video or other content that might be valuable.

Subscription to social accounts. 'Follows', 'Subscribes' and 'Likes' are all forms of mailing lists. This is how you at least in part build an audience that you can share content with on your social media accounts. LinkedIn, YouTube, Instagram, Facebook, Twitter are all examples of social or content networks where you can build these audiences. Each of these then exposes the social profile of your audience members, converting unknown and anonymous visitors into a known person with a profile and tendencies that can be marketed to.

Single Sign On. Single sign on is a feature where you can allow a person to sign up for content or software using their existing social login. Common uses are for example to allow a new mobile app or SaaS user to register and sign up using their existing Facebook, Google, LinkedIn or Twitter profile. These can be effective conversion tool to take anonymous visitors into known prospects so that you're generating leads and then you can begin the process of helping deliver additional content. This also makes registration for your offering easier for the customer, eliminating the need to create yet another account or profile in the digital universe.

Another tool to gain **subscribers** is by producing an opt-in email newsletter. Maybe all first time or returning visitors can be prompted to 'keep getting the type of content you've found here' by entering their email contact into a a pop-up web form. Your website says "Here's some free content. If you'd like to receive more free content in the future, subscribe to our email newsletter." This can be another effective means of taking an anonymous visitor and turning them into an opted-in prospect.

Create a Schedule

The old adage is that if you're failing to plan then you're planning to fail. So create a plan of action. Figure out when you're going to produce which content, events like webinars, how you're going to translate this into leads.

Map out the conversion plan

How do you get an anonymous person to identify themselves? Do you give them content, services, or other lead magnets? What tools do you use to capture their information so they become a known quantity and then how will you help them along their buying journey? How will you create feedback loops in CRM or your Marketing Automation platform to gauge where they are in their buying journey?

Lead Scoring and Grading

A major challenge between Sales and Marketing is always the quality of leads that marketing generates. If marketing is generating lots of apparent interest in content, lead magnets, but these are never turning into anything of significance, who's to blame. Sales or Marketing? Maybe you just want or need to see results from your content and lead generation efforts and grading and scoring seems like an unimportant topic.

The use of Marketing Automation to score or grade leads becomes important then to help really figure out what's going on with prospective clients without engaging in a 1:1 discussion with them.

This is a topic that marketers could write their own voluminous books about if you asked them. I think for the purposes of this discussion it's important to really understand some of the logic behind Scoring v.s. Grading and to come up with a game plan around this in the short term for your business.

Lead Scoring is about tracking the activity of your potential buyers. What content of yours are they consuming? Where are they in the buying cycle? I will also provide a few links of content from various sources that I think might be useful. Lead Scoring in marketing automation is often expressed in a numeric score that is accumulated for a given prospect profile over time as they visit web pages, download content, fill in forms, visit your social profiles.

"Lead scoring is a methodology shared by sales and marketing that ranks leads to determine their sales-readiness. Leads are scored based on interest they show in your business, place in the buying cycle, and overall fit with your business."

Source: The Big List of Lead Scoring Rules, Marketo

Below is an example of a lead scoring matrix that your marketing team might build when configuring your Marketing Automation platform of choice (assuming they are scoring and grading leads).

141

Activity	Points
Form/Landing Page Submission	+5
Submitted "Contact Me" Form	+25
Received an Email	0
Email Open	+1
Email Clickthrough	+3
Registered for Webinal	+3
Attended Webinar	+10
Downloaded a Document	+5
Visited a Landing Page	+2
Unsubscribed from Newsletter	-2
Watched a Demo	+8
Contact is a CXO	+5
Visited Trade Show Booth	+3
Visited Pricing Page	+10

Source: 3 Best practices Creating Lead Scoring, Act On

Lead Grading by contrast can be used in conjunction with Lead Scoring to improve the understanding of where a given prospect is and whether it's time for sales to connect with them.

"Lead grading, which is reflected as a letter grade, looks at the flip side of lead scoring: how interested are you in your leads? By comparing each lead's demographic data to your ideal prospect profile (including industries, job titles, company size, and more), you can determine whether or not the lead will be a good fit for your product. This prevents sales reps from wasting their time on leads who ultimately have no intention of making a purchase."

Source:Lead Scoring and Lead Grading Scenarios Explained, Pardot

When you're determining what marketing automation platform to buy, it's going to be important to understand if it has an approach to lead scoring and lead grading.

The above distinctions may not be 100% universal from one platform to another as you might discover when you start comparing Pardot to Marketo to HubSpot or Reply.io, etc. The criteria, however, is logically consistent and whatever you buy, it's important to make sure it's consistent with the lead scoring and grading criteria your marketing expert decides determines the value of a lead. You may also initially decide that every lead is a good lead and someone should follow up on leads by email or phone calls.

That might work initially, but as your efforts become more sophisticated (assuming they do), lead grading and scoring will come into play. You could of course also start out with a more simplistic marketing automation approach, e.g. maybe you use MailChimp or Reply.io and then need to graduate to Marketo or Pardot.

In either case, here are some of the examples of criteria you can grade leads by. These relate to a contact, others may relate to the Account (Company, Organization) a contact works for their relationship to your business e.g. potential partner, customer, employee, etc.

Example of Contact Lead Grading Criteria for Contacts that might be important.

1. Title
2. Role
3. Purchasing authority
4. Number of direct reports
5. Level of manager (to whom do they report?)
6. Years of experience
7. Specialties
8. Type of email used (Gmail, corporate, Yahoo)
9. Years at current position
10. Designations/Certifications

Triggers and Actions

Some marketing automation platforms allow you to use Triggers and Actions to create automated workflow rules, notifications or 'auto generated responses'. Triggers are where something changes in the behavior, status or state of the visitor as recorded in a data field in the contact or lead record. Triggers then kick of some form of Action e.g. an email notification, a task assigned for a person to call the lead etc. These are examples of 'actions'. Email marketing campaigns also might have time-based or action-based replies that can be automated.

Actioning Customer Buying Journeys

An example of how to map out a Customer buying journey and your touch points in that journey is the Salesforce Marketing Cloud Journey Builder. This is where you present content to the visitor, anticipate the meaning behind their consumption of the content and the reply you want to send to them, the action you want them to take. Many marketing automation platforms allow you to take a theoretical buying journey of the prospect and to create it in a digital website, app or landing page.

New Relationship Between Sales and Marketing

"Gone are the days of throwing leads "over the wall" to Sales without responsibility or visibility to when, if, and how those deals are closed, won, or lost. Marketing now has the ability and directive to influence performance throughout the entire funnel, from first contact to close. Thus, the traditional chasm between Sales and Marketing is shrinking by necessity—the two departments have to work together, with firm baton handoffs throughout the sales funnel in order to meet revenue goals for which both are now responsible."

Source: Sales Playbook Business Development, Bulldog Solutions

Account Based Marketing

In business to business sales, ABM or Account Based Marketing refers to targeting specific contacts inside of target businesses that meet a specific profile. The idea is that, depending upon the size, industry, and nature of a target business, they may have multiple potential people inside of the business that can initiate a buying process. The marketer will target people inside of target accounts based upon their title and role and the assumed needs they have using email copy, content, and tactics to engage the right contacts across an account.

This goes hand in hand with Account-Based Selling where the sales team similarly will work a set number of target businesses and try to build relationships with the right people at these businesses.

Identify Stakeholders

1. Executive Sponsor
2. Operational buyer
3. Financial buyer
4. Technical buyer
5. Influencers

3 x 3

Process of matching up appropriate contacts at your business with appropriate contacts at your prospect business and making sure they are having the right type of conversation. Each of the needs of each level will need to be addressed.

1. Executive Buyers: address the business strategy and positioning
2. Management: information and decision making to help implement the strategy and report on it
3. Operational Buyers: day-to-day tactics and problems

Competition

Who are your competitors, what are their strengths and why do customers buy from them? In what ways are your products or services different? Comparing your product or service positioning to a market leader can be effective if you have purposely aligned to customers in a different fashion.

As previously discussed, the best way to deal with competition might be to create some massive differentiation, to do things in a way they cannot. In either case, make sure you know who's in the market and answer the question for prospects ahead of time of why you're different and why your Ideal Client should be buying from your business.

Who is the decision maker?

This is the person at the customer organization that can give the final approval on buying a solution. They sponsor, greenlight, and sign the final contract to move ahead.

Who are the influencers?

In larger or more complex organizations, there may be team members that provide feedback, research and guidance to the decision maker. It's important to understand their organizational role, if they have specific needs that need to be met. Perhaps they just are a trusted advisor with a technological or business understanding the decision maker relies upon.

What is the buying process?

Usually, whether business to business or business to consumer, marketers will engage potential clients at one of four points in their buying process.

The prospect has:
> 1. No Recognition of a Problem

2. Recognizes there is a Problem
3. Searches potential Solutions to their Problem
4. Is evaluating and selecting a Solution from vendors or providers

The earlier a marketing campaign engages prospects in their process, sometimes the better, as they can think like the prospect and provide content and direction as they progress to the point where they are ready to be engaged by sales.

When to Engage Sales

You should of course pass the lead to Sales when they are identified by marketing as a potential buyer. Maybe the buying process is complex and you need a sales person to contact the prospect. Perhaps marketing sends a ready buyer to an e-commerce page to sign up as a new customer.

In the case of direct sales organizations (you have sales people who talk to customers that are getting ready to buy) if marketing passes a prospect that is not ready to engage in a buying process too soon, Sales may punt back an opportunity into marketing. Usually this requires a ready made email nurturing campaign.

Making sure you have the internal resources

What roles do you need to execute your Traffic and Conversion Plan?

1. Growth Hacker - the evil genius who tests, adjusts campaigns, offers to unlock a scalable vertical or segment using marketing automation and content, sometimes product offerings
2. Marketing Coordinator or Manager

3. Social Media Coordinator
4. Email Marketing Manager
5. Web Content Creation and Conversion
6. Product Marketing - who defines your products, service and the reason behind their configuration, pricing and capabilities, features?

Giving Marketing 'A Lead Number'

How will you measure marketing's effectiveness? Today with all the tools and data marketing has potentially at its disposal, the days of throwing dollars away on advertising no one can track the value of seem gone. Instead, we are firmly in an era where marketing can be held accountable for both the volume and quantity of opportunities they bring into your business.

> *"The dysfunctional relationship between Sales and Marketing is the kiss of death in a buyer-driven world."*
>
> Source: HubSpot *Sales Acceleration Formula, Mark Roberge*

In the *Sales Acceleration Formula*, Mark Roberge suggests that marketing provide a "Service Level Agreement" (SLA).

149

> *"Use the Sales and Marketing SLA to replace the subjective and qualitative aspects of the Sales/Marketing relationship with well-defined targets and qualified goals."*
>
> Source: HubSpot *Sales Acceleration Formula, Mark Roberge*

The foundation of this SLA is the marketing persona of the buyer. That is the profile/demographics of the defined audience. Each customer type will have different campaigns, content, as well as corresponding conversion and activation rates. So, the Service Level would presumably vary according to these different types because the buying journey and sale process would vary also.

Examples of Small, MidMarket and Enterprise Buyer Persona

Automate and Grow

Small Business Persona

Buyer Journey State	Customer Conversion %	Revenue Per Customer	Lead Value
Problem Education	1%	$40k	$400
Solution Research	5%	$40k	$2,000
Solution Selection	20%	$40k	$8,000

Mid Business Persona

Buyer Journey State	Customer Conversion %	Revenue Per Customer	Lead Value
Problem Education	2%	$200k	$4,000
Solution Research	6%	$200k	$12,000
Solution Selection	25%	$200k	$50,000

Enterprise Persona

Buyer Journey State	Customer Conversion %	Revenue Per Customer	Lead Value
Problem Education	3%	$700k	$21,000
Solution Research	10%	$700k	$70,000
Solution Selection	30%	$700k	$210,000

Product Marketing: What about products and services?

While the creation and development of your products, services or software offering might be left to other groups in your business like engineering, manufacturing, development or creative teams, marketing should play a key role in creating a winning product definition and positioning.

Marketing first should help by defining your offering. What problem does your product or service solve? What features do you deliver? How does this benefit the Ideal Client? What are the alternatives they could choose and why would they choose you or your solution to their problem?

A great product these days may not have all the features under the sun, but perhaps it's better to have a unique offering with a clear message to a specific client. Do one thing that others do not in the exact fashion that you do.

Who is in charge of creating products that match Ideal Client needs?

You want a team member really dedicated to building a unique offering around your company's mission and vision.

Get Feedback

Asking questions of potential customers around their problems, ideal solutions can reveal to a product marketing team leader the answers around creating unique product and service offerings. You want someone to be finely attuned to deliver on underlying needs enough not to just create orders, but to have a strategy around product and service creation.

The process of asking these questions can include:

1. Taking a customer to lunch

2. Sending a survey
3. Sending quizzes
4. Providing a Free Gift in each for feedback forms being completed
5. Meeting with your executives for discovery session, like bringing in a VP or Founder of your company to meet with executives at the client company

Keep in mind that the needs of a customer may vary according to the role a person plays in that customer's company.

Executives - think in terms of strategy
Directors/VP - think in terms of overall company objectives
Managers and frontline Employees - think in terms of day-to-day systems, processes and procedures

When considering each type of feedback to see if there are product or service opportunities and insights, you will want to evaluate customer feedback then to understand:

1. Who has the problem? What is their role and will the customer pay to solve the problem?
2. How many people does this affect?
3. Do competitors solve this problem?
4. What is the cost of this problem to the customer in terms of operational, financial or other pain?
5. What is value of solving this problem? What are the benefits to their business?
6. What would the solution look like?
7. What would the cost to your business be to solve this pain?
8. What would the potential benefits to your company be? Increased revenues? Retention?

How Flexible Can You Be?

Depending upon your business, creating new offerings may be more or less challenging. Understand this process in your own business. Services, content and information products may be easier to create than software, and software may be easier to create than hard goods. Have a realistic view of the creation of products, the time, cost and the potential return on investment having a responsive product development cycle.

The product is a huge part of the experience your customer has.

Aside from our relationship with the customer, i.e. how we communicate with and treat them, if we can create awesome products, services and applications, we can attract and retain customers. 'Me too' products, poorly positioned, poorly executed services and software, or poorly distinguished products can have the opposite effect. You can repel customers with a terrible offering.

Who builds the product?

Is this hard good, soft good, service or software application? Do you have the people internally who can engineer, design and deliver on the features and solution?

Digital Products or Services

Even if your company sells hard goods, physical products or services, adding Digital products or Services can drive new revenues, customer loyalty or
155

retention. This includes creating digital customer portals, software, mobile applications on iPhone or Android. It can include tracking, information and reporting products or features.

Up-Selling

Product marketing needs to define the product features and prices. You can attract customers with freemium or entry level products or services and then up sell the client by demonstrating value using videos or articles at the point of purchase. Are there add on products or services. Think in terms of an immediate way to increase the value of the sale. This is easiest for digital products, services or products that you are directing through an e-commerce sign up process.

How to Implement Your Traffic and Conversion Plan - The Team

The people you hire to attack your marketing will be critical in both the creation of your traffic and conversion plan and equally important in its execution and refinement over time. There are options and considerations when we build a marketing team. Sometimes you can hire internally for the specific roles or there can also be external options.

Get Outside Help

If you do not have the internal expertise to execute upon or even create a Traffic and Conversion plan you can hire a contractor or freelancer. Using sites like Upwork.com or Guru.com or even Fivver.com, you can find on demand help for technology, development, marketing, sales or other functions.

The availability of freelancers and the ability to outsource work is an amazing tool for our business. Full-time employees are not a necessity today. Often, you can gain the skills you need on either a permanent or temporary basis from a capable and skilled digital freelancer. Just be very specific around the tools you want to use, the skills you need and the expectations for some form of outcome from the freelancer's time and effort.

Hire a Consultant

Consultants are another level of finding outside help. You can find individual or group of consultants who have expertise and a system in a particular area. Product marketing? SEO? Email Marketing? Lead Generation. There are consultants for these and more.

Hire an Agency

Agencies are another avenue to acquire outside expertise and help. Agencies differ in that they will have ideas, expertise and multiple team resources including, but not limited to, team resources providing creative, technical, managerial, project management skill sets. Agencies often also come with their own marketing technology for email, social and content.

Buy a 'Done-for-You' Service

Another option is to buy a done for you packaged service. This is where you hire a packaged lead generation, marketing or other service that has a definite fixed or monthly cost for a specific deliverable.

157

How can you get people to work for you for less or free, while unleashing their creative genius upon your business?

The concept of crowdsourcing is one of the exponential organization tools that Peter Diamandis, the X prize founder and founder of Singularity University, talks about in his book *Abundance: The Future Is Better Than You Think*.

By unleashing the genius of crowds, you can achieve a number of ends including design, product innovation, data mining, data analysis and even promotion of your business. Here are a few examples of platforms or approaches of this.

Tongal is a crowdsourced studio. Founded in 2009 in Santa Monica, the company maintains an online platform that connects businesses in need of creative work with an online community of writers, directors, and production companies

99 Designs is a graphic design company that creates logos, websites, applications, business cards, book covers, vehicle wraps, and more.

Kickstarter is a public benefit corporation. People who back Kickstarter projects are offered tangible rewards or experiences in exchange for their pledges.[6] This model traces its roots to subscription model of arts patronage, where artists would go directly to their audiences to fund their work.

Hackathons are competitive events in which app and computer developers -- and others involved in software development, including graphic designers, interface designers, project managers, and others, often including subject-matter-experts, collaborate intensively on software projects. The goal of holding a hackathon is generally to create usable software.

Crowdflower is a data mining and crowdsourcing company based in San Francisco, United States. The company offers a software as a service which allows users to access an online workforce to clean, label and enrich data.

Kaggle is a platform for predictive modelling and analytics competitions in which companies and researchers post data and statisticians and data miners compete to produce the best models for predicting and describing the data. This crowdsourcing approach relies on the fact that there are countless strategies that can be applied to any predictive modeling task and it is impossible to know at the outset which technique or analyst will be most effective.

Expert Interview Brian Wright, LeadMD

Brian Wright is a certified Marketo expert specializing in first time integrations of marketing automation platforms and CRM. He is a Marketing Consultant with LeadMD. LeadMD is the original Marketo services partner and has worked with half of all Marketo users in one way or another.

MD: How important is it to use a marketing automation platform like Marketo today for businesses?

Brian Wright: I think that just about every business out there would benefit from marketing automation in some shape or form. That being said, marketing automation is often seen as this magic bullet that will solve an organization's marketing woes, provide new leads by the bucketfull and add visibility and reporting that wasn't possible before - truth is, it just doesn't work like that. My dad always told me that there are few things in life that are more satisfying than having the perfect tool for a job. Of course he was talking about a 3/4" socket and not a SaaS product but the metaphor still holds true. Marketing automation is just another tool in a marketer's tool belt and like any good tool it must be used correctly to be successful. The companies that are getting the most out of their marketing automation tools are the ones that acknowledge that marketing maturity is a process that starts with proper strategy, proper planning and the right people and are willing to invest the time it takes to make it successful.

MD: If I am a start-up or even an existing small to medium sized business; what do I need to do before I dive into marketing automation?

Brian Wright: Marketing automation is all about scaling effort by creating processes which can be replicated. It's about identifying those processes in a business that involve resources or time that can be replicated and governed with a set of rules. The big challenge for many business with marketing automation is that their business processes aren't strong enough or are too complicated to replicate within the tool. Much of my job as a consultant is spent helping companies either shore-up business processes or remove complexity to the point at which we can introduce automation and efficiency.

MD: Outside consultant or full time marketing automation hire? In your mind, what makes more sense?

Brian Wright: : 99% of the time I would recommend an outside consultant over a full time hire because of the wealth of best practice knowledge that a consultant brings to the table. There are people out there that have the tools and skills necessary to be a great full-time marketing automation hire but we call them marketing unicorns for a reason. Working with a consultant or team of consultants allows you to focus on the big picture business problems that marketing automation needs to solve while allowing for a team to work out the problem and build the structure that enables you for long-term success. In my opinion, there's just no way to replicate the thousands of client instances a consultant worth their salt has seen and worked within while solving problems. That experience is completely invaluable and in many cases after we've helped with an implementation or health check on an org, we'll help the client find the right full time marketing automation hire for long term success.

MD: Does it matter what industry I am in? Can I leverage marketing automation?

Brian Wright: Some industries are more ripe for marketing automation than others but I do feel that all companies, regardless of industry can benefit from marketing automation in some form or another. Even companies with very hands-on sales processes can benefit from automated emails to current customers containing case studies or recent accomplishments if for no purpose other than staying top of mind. You want to reach your customers where they are spending their time, so if that's on email then you want to be distributing some good content via email on a regular cadence. If your customers are only acquired via tradeshows or direct mail then fine, just configure your marketing automation tool to track those costs and the return on that investment.

MD: What are the 2-3 most important types of digital marketing activities that I need to be investing in every day?

Brian Wright:
1. Your website- every company worth doing business with should have a website that allows customers to understand what they're about, what they're selling and how to reach them and do business with them. The website should, at the bare minimum, instill confidence that the company is trustworthy and provide a way to convert that viewer into a known lead with a name, email address, phone number, company name, etc. These conversion points on your website, whether it's a newsletter sign-up or a contact us form, should be optimized and reported on by a digital marketing on a weekly, monthly, quarterly basis against the cost of running the website to develop insight into acquisition cost.
2. Campaign- a marketing campaign can be anything from sending of automated emails via

Constant Contact or other marketing automation tool or paid advertising via google adwords or facebook ads Like I said previously, reach your customers where they are spending their time ... this could be trade magazines, trade shows, social media, you name it there's a way for you to market via that channel. Which brings me to the 3rd point:

3. Find a way to report on anything you're spending money on. Work hard to understand key metrics around lead acquisition cost, customer acquisition cost and lifetime value of a customer. These metrics help you determine how your current marketing campaigns are performing and if any new channel or campaign you may add into the mix perfoms against already established baselines.

MD: What do you think of Marketing committing to Service Level Agreements? e.g. generate a certain number of leads, quality of leads etc. over time.

Brian Wright: I think marketing committing to SLA's is a great way to make sure that marketing and sales are kept in alignment and that each side upholds their end of the bargain. Historically, only the sales side has been held to SLAs and with the new push towards Account Based Marketing we're seeing more and more commitments from the marketing side of the house towards SLA's.

Chapter Summary Points
1. A Traffic and Conversion plan will outline your target Ideal Clients, digital marketing channels your tactics to attract, activate and convert them into customers

2. Marketing Automation is the use of software to automate and scale this process
3. It is important when creating your traffic and conversion plan to attribute a Service Level Agreement between marketing and sales around lead quantity, quality and conversion.
4. Product Marketing may also be a function you implement. This can play a critical role in gathering information around new target segments products, features, services or software that can be created to leverage digital technology like apps and software to achieve growth.

References
https://en.wikipedia.org/wiki/Growth_hacking
https://www.quicksprout.com/the-definitive-guide-to-growth-hacking/
https://blog.hubspot.com/marketing/resources-master-marketing-automation-under-100
https://www.amazon.com/Start-Why-Leaders-Inspire-Everyone/dp/1591846447
https://www.act-on.com/blog/3-best-practices-creating-lead-scoring-matrix/
http://events.bulldogsolutions.com/KnowledgeBase/SalesPlaybookBD.pdf
http://searchengineland.com/guide/what-is-paid-search
http://www.pardot.com/blog/4-lead-scoring-and-grading-scenarios-explained
https://www.youtube.com/watch?v=zAVxI5wWGKU 44:11
https://www.marketo.com/worksheets/the-big-list-of-lead-scoring-rules/
Marketo downloadable checklist at:
https://www.marketo.com/worksheets/the-big-list-of-lead-scoring-rules/

Chapter 6: Building Out Your Sales Capability

Before we begin investing in sales automation technology, we need to build a plan, a blueprint for your sales organization that defines how you will sell to customers.

This playbook can be adjusted over time, but it will be critical to your growth and when we are defining what processes and data collection to automate during the sales process. It will also be a critical document to use when educating new team members so they understand their roles in the overall sales process.

While a lot of this is, at first glance, focused upon a playbook for a direct sales model, you can easily adapt this to address an e-commerce sales model.

Let's move on to talk about the nature of your customer.

Business to Business, or Business to Consumer?

The first thing to define is what segment you're selling to, Business to Business (B2B) or Business to Consumer (B2C)? This is important because your sales process and your customer's buying journey will differ based upon how you answer this question.

If you're selling to consumers, we're focused upon individuals and households. If we're selling to businesses, then we need to understand things like the industry, business size, business problem we're addressing, decision makers and the steps in a more complex sales cycle.

Ideal Customer

The second question we need to understand is, who is our Ideal Customer? We defined this when we created our Traffic and Conversion plan. There may be more than one.

This should also give us a clue as to the channels we'll sell to customers in. Channels are the way that we bring products to a customer. Within each channel, we'll have a defined sales process that will have steps the customer typically takes during their customer journey.

A part of how we interact with each customer will be the Key Messages that we need to be communicated to the Customer.

This Key Message for each customer and in each channel includes your Story of What you do, How you do it that is unique, and Why you decided to tackle a problem that this customer has.

Our playbook will state some important things:
1. Customer Profile
2. Offering to each customer
3. Sales Channel(s)
4. Key messages to Customer
5. Sales Team in each channel
6. Stages of the Sales Process in each Channel.

Automating Different Sales Processes

When we talk about Sales Automation, there are really two types of sales in my mind these days.

1. **E-commerce:** some sort of transaction that is self-initiated by a customer. This can be

through a website, a landing page, pushing a button, adding items to a cart. Whatever the case, the customer has been led through their buying journey sufficiently and made a digital offer and are ready to buy. By its very nature, this type of Sale is automated to one extent or another

2. **Direct sales:** this is where you have one or more human resources that help the customer past the qualification stage of being a suspect or lead. They are now a prospect or a customer with a Sales Opportunity. There is budget, timing and the need to solve a problem. The customer needs help to fill in the gaps and to get to the point where they sign a contract or request a sale of some sort. This may be a higher ticket sale, a business to business sale to large or more complex organizations. Software, services, consulting, hard goods, whatever the case, there is sufficient financial opportunity to justify a few different people working on sales opportunities that may stretch out over a longer buying journey than a more transactional immediate sale. The relationship and communication of human to human contact pays off and is needed.

Or possibly your approach to selling is some hybrid of the two, where parts of the sales process are automated and/or via e-commerce, but you have direct sales team members helping customers along. The types of automation in the second scenario differ from the first, but there is still plenty of opportunity to automate parts of the sales process.

167

Regardless of a digital or direct sales channel, the information system at the core of either type of channel will be some sort of **Customer Relationship Management** (CRM) application.

> "Like a game-day playbook to a quarterback, sales playbooks can provide the pivotal next move to a salesperson. They can shorten sales cycles, increase win rates, ramp up new salespeople, bolster deal sizes and optimize overall sales performance. In other words, they help salespeople win."
>
> Source: How To Write A Killer Sales Playbook, Qvidian

How Do You Write a Killer Sales Playbook?

While the selling methods may vary, a Sales playbook provides you with a valuable 'living' document to onboard new sales reps, document your sales process and approach to customer needs, objections and competitive factors. This can also apply to digital commerce where you provide the framework for electronic commerce build out.

Once you have a sales playbook in place you can also leverage this to customize your CRM. This allows you to implement the stages of your sales process for each opportunity, create workflow rules and assignments to guide reps around next steps to advancing complex deals. You can create cues for reps to outreach at appropriate intervals across a set of accounts and implement sales reports that matter to management.

Your sales playbook should have contributions from sales leaders that mirror the actual engagement of real life customers. If circumstances change (market, competition or approaches to customer needs), the sales playbook can then be easily updated along with your technology tools like CRM.

Here are some common components you should include in your sales playbook. For a template, consider downloading ours here:

http://www.automateandgrow.biz/salesplaybook

"Sales playbooks are a means of capturing sales best practices and communicating them to salespeople. They concisely describe what a salesperson should do in different situations. Although not a substitute for comprehensive training, a good sales playbook is a valuable resource salespeople and B2B marketing professionals can use to recall and implement best practices in real-time."

Source: Marketo: Marketing and Sales Alignment

Playbook Components

1. **Customer analysis** – Identifies the market, key trends, key buyers and influencers, a profile of the ideal customer, the customer's pain points and preferences and the critical business issues customers are trying to solve.

2. **Buying process** – Identifies conditions or events that trigger consideration, evaluation, and purchase. What are the behaviors of a qualified lead?

169

3. **Company offer and value proposition** – Describes and clarifies what your company offers and the ways in which your products and services address the customer's pain points and business issues.

4. **Story of Why** – This is the place to explain why your company exists and how your company makes a difference to the customer and in the market. This section of the playbook is not complete until it answers two questions. First, "Why should people buy this product from you?" Second, "What is the value they receive buying this product from you?" Part of this section should be dedicated to giving examples of questions that draw out the customer's business needs and pain points. This section is also a good place to include use-case scenarios.

5. **Value propositions** – This is where you explain how your product solves customers' problems or improves their situation (relevancy), delivers specific benefits (quantified value), tells the ideal customer why they should buy from you and not from the competition (unique differentiation).

6. **Competitive analysis** – Details how competitors position themselves in the market, their selling process, typical moves by each competitor, and recommendations on how to counter these moves.

7. **Sales Methodology** – Maps the customer buying process, and outlines your sales process, that is, the standard set of critical steps that moves the customer to buy. While this section should outline the sales cycle

stages and responsibilities, it should go beyond just describing the steps in the sales cycle. It should provide instructions on what information needs to be collected at each stage in the process, identify the players in each step, and how to assess the opportunity.

How Do You Define Your Sales Process?

Most sales processes provide milestones or stages that align with the customer buying process. Typical sales processes, however, include some variation of the following:

- Qualification
- Discovery & Needs Analysis
- Presentation of Capabilities and Solutions
- Proposal
- Negotiation
- Close for Win/Lose

For your sales playbook, you will want to articulate for each of these (or other) stages, a description of the stage, outcomes and milestones that complete a stage or lead to the next stage.

"The difference between a high-performing sales team and a sales team that struggles to meet its numbers is process. With only 46% of forecasted deals closing, the importance of a trackable and repeatable sales process is paramount. Teams with a clear and consistent process are more likely to move deals through the pipeline consistently and close them cleanly."

Source: Using Sales Playbooks That Align With The Buyers Journey, Jennifer Earl & Steve Haverdick Revegy

8. The **Opportunity Assessment** information should recommend standard methods and tools that help determine where customers are in the buying process, enable them to analyze the situation, and anticipate what they might do next. This section of the playbook should also provide the guidelines for entering and exiting opportunities and a list of the resources, skills, knowledge, and tools needed for each stage in the process.

9. **Countering objections** – Gives specific instruction on how to address each common objection sales might encounter. Tom Reilly takes a look at this topic in his book, *Value-Added Selling : How to Sell More Profitably, Confidently, and Professionally by Competing on Value, Not Price*.

10. **Best practices** – Lists proven tips, techniques—and under what circumstances to use them. This section should also capture what hasn't worked in the past and associated lessons learned.

11. **Target Verticals and/or Accounts** – These are specific lists of named accounts or named Verticals.

12. **Your Buyer Personae** – A section (perhaps an appendix) that answers the question, "Who is my ideal prospect?" Vertical specific buyer personas (including objections, pain points, journeys, etc. for each one) or even Vertical specific user personas should be included here.

13. **Internal Org chart** – how are your sales, marketing, support and business operations teams organized?

14. **Sales territory breakdown/alignment** – who inside of the sales team does what and how are they aligned to target accounts, market segments or verticals?

16. **Product demos** – do you provide these? If so, what are the criteria that reps can arrange demos and what is the process to submit a request? Are there agreements the customer must sign or is there (ideally) an online enrollment that converts into a paying customer account?

17. **Market segments** – Define the criteria you use to segment your customers. This is where we divide a broad consumer or business market (both existing and prospects) into groups. These are known as segments. The criteria is based on some type of common characteristics.

18. **Use cases** – What are the applications of your products or services? How do these vary by customer type or market segment?

"60% of B2B companies lack a well-defined sales process, so putting one in place now will give you the competitive advantage you need to grow your business. It will enable your reps to hit each milestone required before progressing

a deal forward before its ready and as a result, will increase your lead-to-customer close rates."
Source: Sales Process Cheatsheet, Hubspot

19. **Customer profiles** – Who are your existing customers? What are their segmented characteristics? Use this to define customer persona - a general grouping of your customers under a fictional persona for each so there is a defined example of what a customer looks like, what their needs are.

20. **Content overview** – (how it relates to each persona) – Marketing builds customer persona, but sales probably has more direct content sources that apply to each persona and market segment. What types of content do you want sales teams sending? The same can apply to e-commerce guided customers and there is a touch point here that should be defined between sales and marketing. Who sends the content in what campaign, what are the triggers to alert SDRs to follow up on content consumption? What about webinars? What about video creation and consumption? The follow-up and campaigns for each of these may require different defined practices

21. **Sales and Marketing SLA** (if there's an SLA with inbound leads, what's the cadence?)

22. **Salesforce.com/CRM training** – define what teams need to be trained in CRM, what the best practices are around each sales team role.

23. **Lead statuses and definitions** – For example, status sometimes includes Open,

Working, Closed-Converted, Closed-Not Converted.

24. **Funnel stages and definitions** – These should mirror sales process steps like Qualified, Presentation, Proposal, Negotiation, Closed-Won, Closed-Lost, On Hold.

25. **Lead handoff process** – What is the criteria that determines when leads move from Marketing to Sales Development Reps to BDRs or Account Executives? What tasks and actions need to occur at each step?

26. **Prospecting best practices** – For Business Development Representatives, this can include a cold email outreach, LinkedIn add, sending content, phone calls or invitations to webinars or live events. What needs are they trying to uncover, what questions should they be asking? How often and over how many days do BDRs connect with prospects?

27. **Expectations** of team members by role and responsibility, vertical. This includes how many leads they handle every day or week; how many they convert (SDRs for example). It includes turnaround time on follow up (what steps of this are automated, which require a rep to take action.) For BDRs this can include how many new targeted contacts or accounts they reach out to each day. What percentage are targeted as being converted. For Account Executives, there may be how many Accounts they handle, how many monthly opportunities they manage. They may have quotas around

revenue including new, retained and growth within named Accounts.

"A successful sales playbook is a living document that serves as a roadmap for sales leaders and teams throughout the sales process. It's also a valuable tool for on-boarding new salespeople, a central repository for ongoing training, and a guide for handing off new customers to post-sale teams."

Source:
http://labs.openviewpartners.com/hubspot-sales-playbook-tips/

What is CRM?

Customer Relationship Management (CRM) software has been around for a very long time.

Maybe once upon a time (let's call this time the pre-information age), this was the rolodex a sales rep or company had of contacts, prospects. This gave way increasingly over the last 25 years to some form of database application that keeps track of interactions with prospects and customers.

CRM has evolved over time from a 'desktop' software application to more centralized shared applications. You may have heard of Symantec's "Act CRM," for example which was a particularly successful brand of desktop CRM software in the 1990s. Other names may come to mind, like Goldmine or Maximizer. For larger companies, these gave way to "computerized network" versions of CRM like Siebel or Oracle that are shared or accessible by multiple or groups of users.

Since 1999, the concept of Software as a Service has taken over these older models led by

Salesforce.com who deliver a CRM application via a web browser, mainly. This is killing the client-server, on premise and even data center hosted versions of CRM in the market. Now any business can adopt a SaaS like Salesforce, with APIs, development tools, applications and business function focused add-ons.

There are also many smaller CRM competitors such as Insightly, SugarCRM, ZoHo, Prosperworks, HonchoCRM (full disclosure: that's a plug for a newer product that I have been involved with as an investor.

Regardless of which CRM you choose, there are some core concepts. How we customize and automate sales is we choose a CRM that will allow us to create a system that collects the right information, reports on this, and automates steps in the sales process.

Common CRM concepts are the concept of
- Account (Company)
- Contact (People)
- Deal or Opportunity
- Leads

Within each of these common concepts - often referred to as "objects," there are fields. So, going forward when we reference an object we mean a category or "silo" of data. Within this silo of data ("the object") we collect fields. In the CRM, there are standard fields and we can add custom fields that match the data collection needs of your business. For example, an Account object has fields of data and every time we create a new record on a Company we sell to, we can store data in these fields.

Accounts/Companies/Organizations

This is usually a customer who has bought from you in the past or a potential customer that will buy from you. In most CRMs, an Account is a business. Depending upon the business size or industry it may have multiple locations. In any case, in CRM this object is a collection of fields or information that you would collect on the company.

This may include fields like:

- Company Name
- Company Address
- Phone Number
- Website
- Email.

You may collect the type of customer this Company is relative to your business. You may also want to collect information on the industry of the business, it's approximate employee count and revenue as common data field examples.

All of this and more information will become important as you integrate the data collection not just from Sales but also Marketing and Customer Support. Also, as you begin to rate and grade your accounts according to their quality and categories.

Accounts (we will use this going forward as synonymous with business or company) will also have a one to many relationship to other data objects in the CRM. This usually includes but is not limited to:

- Contacts
- Opportunities

Contacts/People

Assuming you're in a business to business sales engagement, you will have multiple contacts or people you communicate with at an Account.

Within your CRM, we will typically have fields such as First Name, Last Name, Phone Number, Email, Role (Title), maybe the address of the Contact.

You will also, depending upon the CRM, have a history of appointments, tasks, emails, phone calls, notes about the Contact.

Deals/Opportunities

Again, in a B2B type sale, an Opportunity may stretch out over a period of time. This is a potential sale and at its core a Sales Opportunity (or Deal) tracks the steps a sales team or person takes from the point of qualification to the point of closing the sale.

This is where we keep track of fields in the CRM such as the Value in dollars of the Opportunity, the expected date when the salesperson thinks the sale will close, the stage in the sales process where the Opportunity is, the key contact people associated with the Opportunity and even the Products (another record in some CRMs) and pricing that are being discussed in the Opportunity.

Leads vs. Opportunities

These are unqualified Companies and Opportunities. This is usually, for example, where marketing may have a lead generation campaign and someone opts into a list.

179

They may or may not be ready to be a customer. There is usually some process to vet out the level of interest and how far along they are in their buying journey. The success rate that marketing gets at scoring leads and gathering information before passing leads to sales should improve over time.

Sometimes out of the gate this is the first hand-off between marketing and sales on new Accounts or Opportunities. In this object, we're collecting information that will be used to "convert" into an Account, Contact and/or Opportunity record.

Usually in CRM, Leads are a stand-alone record. They do not relate to Accounts, Contacts or Opportunities until they convert. Then, the Lead record archives (disappears from view of the user.) This "conversion" activity is usually an important report in CRM, showing how many leads were qualified and converted by your sales efforts into active Opportunities.

What if You are Selling to Consumers?

If you're focused upon selling to individuals, the concept of an Account may be foreign to your business. For non-profits, for example, raising money and using CRM to track this activity, they may not be raising money from corporate donors.

In these instances, we see two things:

1. The Account can be a household. For example, is there more than one buyer in the household? Maybe the Account is called the Addams Family. The contacts are the husband Gomez, the wife Morticia, the Butler Lurch, etc.

2. The other concept that exists in some CRMs is a Person Account. This is typically an option in Salesforce.com, probably the fastest growing SaaS-based CRM in the world.

This changes the Account to be centered around an individual. So instead of treating the account like a business, you collect information about the individual in this record.

Things that are common to Automate in B2B Sales organizations

Here is a useful list of items that you typically will want to create an automation for in your CRM.

Web to Lead Forms

What if someone submits an inquiry via your website? Who handles this? Where does it go to notify someone to reply? How do you track the follow from this? Typically, we recommend that web-based inquiries are followed up by Sales unless this is a support issue. This is where you would create a new Lead in CRM using a web to lead form. Some CRMs have this as a standard feature e.g. Salesforce has a web-to-lead code feature. Others may require you to create a third-party automation using something like Zapier.com, Formstack.com, Wufoo.com, etc.

Lead Assignments

When new leads come in, they usually identify the source of the lead; for example, if the Lead came from a marketing campaign, if it came from a web to lead form, if it came via a raw list, etc. You can automate the follow-up process by creating assignment rules or queues in many CRMs.

This is where you would create a rule, for example, using a workflow rule or a Zapier.com Zap. The rule might assign the Lead record based upon the source (this is common). Salesforce.com can create a Queue of users and to assign the Lead record to the queue. Then, whoever grabs it out of the queue is then responsible for qualifying that lead.

Lead assignment rules can also be based upon fields, e.g., let's say there is a lead field called Product Interest. If a new Lead comes in, workflow automations can be created to route specific Leads related to a product to a specific CRM user.

Updating the Stage of an Opportunity

Generally, there are common sales stages for each Sales Opportunity that you will establish based upon your Sales Process. Common stages are Qualification, Presentation, Quotation, Negotiation and the Close. This results in a status on Opportunities of: 'active, hold, won, lost.' In most CRMs you can modify these based upon your company's defined process and typical customer interactions.

Stages are often updated manually by Salespeople. In most modern sales organizations there may be a division of sales labour also. For example Sales Development Reps may be responsible for qualification and presentation to a prospect. They would update as they progress an Opportunity through these stages.

A change in stage however can be a trigger to automate re-assignment or a notification to either that sales team member to do something "next". It can also be a trigger for an automation such as an automatic email notification either internally or externally.

For example, let's say there is a division of labor between SDRs and Account Executives where AEs only interact with an Opportunity after a specific qualification process and now the SDR needs the AE to make a presentation to the client. When the SDR updates to the "Presentation Stage" we can use the change in this common field in many CRMs to

- Notify the AE using a task to contact the client
- Automatically send an email to the client to schedule a presentation with the AE

This is just an example but a common one.

It illustrates how we can use fields as triggers and then actions in CRM to create immediate or automatic follow up using emails, tasks, appointments.

Assigning Tasks & Appointments

Many CRMs have the concept of a "task" or "appointment". These are common actions in CRMs like Salesforce.com where a field change may act as the trigger, then we want a human being to do something (call, email, complete some next action, etc.) so we can auto generate a task based upon some rule set. We used an example above.

By assigning a task this gives a *to do* to a human being, and it also gives us reportable information so we can see how many of a particular type of task were assigned. Tasks may have a "type" field. For example, maybe the Task type = send email. Great, so we could report for any particular AE all of the new Tasks they were assigned where type = email. Then the task has a status usually, like "in progress or complete".

Tasks can be an important way to understand the day-to-day activities of salespeople. Sometimes, just judging or evaluating someone on outcomes (e.g. closed-won, closed-lost Opportunities) is not enough. What are they doing each day? Are they sending emails? Are they closing tasks to call clients? This is the value of assigning and reporting on tasks.

Similarly, in many CRMs, for Appointments, you can see how many of a type of appointment a salesperson has. These too can be categorized using fields like type and status.

For example, what about an Appointment "type"- needs analysis? This might be a type of appointment where a discovery of the client's needs is done and information is collected by the sales rep to further assess what options to present to the client.

You get the idea. CRM becomes the central point where we assign and track the outcomes on sales activities now.

Quotations

Do your customers require quotations? This often involves a few things: the product, the pricing, the terms and conditions.

Some CRMs offer this as a feature. Many require an add-on license or third-party solution to automate and even digitize Quotations.

Cash to Quote is increasingly the description given to the functionality where sales reps can configure product offers, prices and conditions.

Cash to Quote or CPQ applications not only generate an electronic quote in CRM that can be sent to the client, but they will also allow your team to create digital approval processes. For example, maybe you require a special price to win a deal. This could be accomplished by triggering a workflow approval request from a salesperson to finance or a manager or other executive before the quote is sent electronically to the customer.

Maybe you require particular products to be bundled. How do you ensure that these rules are automated and built into your CRM quotation process? Building product rules is often a feature of Cash to Quote solutions, like Salesforce CPQ, Apptus or Oracle CPQ Cloud.

Once you determine the pricing and product configuration, how do you get the client approval?

This too can be automated using e-signature integrations such as DocuSign, Adobe or SignNow. You can send an electronic document by email to your client; they review and accept it by signing the contract digitally. When this is signed, in your CRM this notifies the rep and perhaps other internal resources that, hey - we have a sale. Often this then kicks off a post-sales fulfillment process. Orders, pick pack and shipping and invoicing, collections.

Orders

Many CRMs have an Order object. An order can be manually created based upon an Opportunity, or in more complex CRMs, you can automatically generate an Order. An order record usually contains details from a converted (closed-won) Opportunity about the agreed to terms, pricing and product configuration that needs to be delivered.

For really advanced CRM implementations, you can manage and track the progress of an order through to invoicing and service/product delivery, again using status and stages of an order.

Invoices

Invoicing is usually done in your company's finance application. For many companies, this might be QuickBooks, FreshBooks or Xero Accounting. For others, they may have a full-blown ERP like SAP/Oracle or Microsoft A/X. Using triggers in more complex CRMs, like Salesforce, or by using an intermediary application like Zapier, you can create rules to trigger the creation of an invoice in an external application. For example, the stage is updated to Closed-Won on an Opportunity. It triggers an Order. If the Order hits its own status of "ready to ship", that status can further be used to send details to, let's call it QuickBooks, to generate an invoice.

Email Communication

Workflow Rules and Triggers can be used to communicate automatically through CRM to a Lead, Contact or Account via email messages. Similar to how we can create automated emails for marketing campaigns, we can trigger notification emails prompting a meeting, an action or approval request using email templates.

For example, you may wish to auto generate a meeting request to a contact when there is a stage change from Qualification to Presentation. This trigger could send an email to the contact on the Opportunity to send an email with the subject "Let's set up a time for a presentation".

That email would then prompt the client maybe to go to a web page connected to the assigned Account Owner (example, an Account Executive) and to select a published calendar time.

You can use applications like YouCanBook.me or Yesware that allow you to publish a calendar and availability for a user on a public webpage. This connects directly into the Google or Outlook calendar of the user.

SMS Text Notifications & Communication

Similarly, it is possible to send text message notifications from CRM to a contact. This is less common but very possible. This may often apply more to consumer-based sales interactions – but who's to say you don't do something similar with business to business? What is more direct than texting a contact? You have a lot of benefits. Platforms like Twilio or Zang.io would potentially allow us to create SMS text interactions from CRM to contact or leads' mobile phones.

Sales Dashboards and Reporting

In most CRMs, it's possible to create reports on all record types (objects) and their fields.

There are some common examples of reports leaders may want including:
- Lead Conversion report
- Opportunity report
- Sales report
- Activity report

If you collect the information, there is a way in most CRMs to report on this. When we meet with customers, you would be shocked at how many reports are based on an Excel spreadsheet.

This is a common time waster for sales, marketing, finance and some pseudo sales support role, often called sales operations, where a person is doing the work of a machine.

For many reasons, it is important to understand what the sales team is forecasting, for example. This gives clues to management and service/product delivery around resources they need to anticipate deploying for projected sales opportunities that look like they will close.

Why is this done in a spreadsheet? Holy crow. Get a CRM that collects and reports on this information.

Dashboards are a way in many CRM apps to "pin" a regular report run to a main screen with a visualization. A bar chart based upon a common Funnel Report could be an example.

Another level beyond simple reports and dashboards might be Business Intelligence (BI). You hear talk of "big data". BI tools like Tableau or Wave Analytics can be used to collect data from CRM, but also from other sources and combine these into powerful predictive analyses.

Calendaring and Email Integration

There are various ways and benefits of integrating a user's Google or Outlook calendar to CRM. This allows for ubiquitous task and appointment synchronization. You can also integrate a user's primary email identity with CRM. This often allows you to track and report on email communications between an SDR, BDR or AE and a Lead or Contact in an Account. This functionality varies CRM to CRM and can be a little complex, believe it or not.

The benefits to the user are that integration of the two can streamline communications rather than hunting and pecking through an email inbox, reps can see the account or person-based communications.

This is not amazing on most CRMs, by the way, but it is important in either case to address this in any CRM setup.

How to Choose a CRM

This is a complicated subject to be honest but I will attempt to provide a starting framework that should be useful.

An array of CRM options exist but when in doubt, Salesforce.com is in my opinion currently the gold standard. It is priced accordingly however, that is not cheap. I believe that unless you're a small or medium sized business Salesforce.com today is almost always the platform to choose.

For any medium to enterprise business I really don't understand choices that are 'on-premise based'. This is where you would host a server with CRM software on the server that is accessed using a client-server networking model. While some vendors offer on premise versions of their CRM for example Oracle, Siebel, Microsoft CRM, the truth is this is adding unnecessary complications to deploying CRM. Someone will really have to pay me a lot of cash to convince me otherwise.

Salesforce.com, by contrast, is always 100% software as a service (SaaS, web based via a browser). They also have the best customization/automation/development platform compared to pretty much any other CRM application from any other vendor.

Microsoft, to me, is in trouble in this space. They are stuck in an old technology stack and no matter how you slice it they don't have a great CRM. They also do not have a great development story, they don't have very good answers around Customer Support or Marketing Automation. Move on.

Oracle can stick to ERP and other complex databases as far as I am concerned. That's big data sets in big giant corporations and years of trying to make it work.

Relative to these options Salesforce is inexpensive. Now, if you're sub-one hundred user business, which I think if you're reading this you likely are, you can decide to shop around.

There are some really good SaaS-based small to mid-market CRM options that all have their own flavor, features and likely pricing and product advantages. If you have the time money and energy to scale it makes sense to invest in Salesforce, but you can decide for yourself.

If you're in a sub one hundred (100) user seat scenario there are options to consider.

Here are roughly the 14 things that I would evaluate.

1. User Interface. Is the software easy to use? Is it visually appealing. This is a good place to start. Is it easy to understand for an untrained user (ideally) the purpose of the software and to start using it right away? If you're evaluating the user interface you want to play with it and decide if it is obvious how to do what you need to do.

Things like layout, labels, colours are important. You presumably will have team members staring at this quite a bit. It will be where they record activity and get information they need to do their job. If the UI is offensively bad, that is 100% going to impact the success or failure of your Sales and maybe Support automation initiatives.

2. Handling of Email. Email is a very important form of business communication, needless to say. We use this not only for marketing efforts but also for proactive sales outreach and even customer support. So how your prospective CRM handles email is important. Does it integrate with your chosen email back end easily? Can you see the email communications between a Contact, Lead or Account and the rep in question?

What can you do inside of CRM that gets recorded in your email inbox/outbox?

Can you see emails recorded as completed tasks? Can you read emails themselves? How important is this? How complicated is it to integrate to Google Mail, Microsoft Exchange or your own IMAP server?

Can you extend email sequences to sales reps? Setting up automated outreach might be a separate function from CRM and require an email specific application but then how do the two applications talk?

3. Customization Story. How can you customize the CRM in question? Some CRMs allow you to add new users, roles and permissions.

They allow you to add custom fields that you need inside of your business to objects (Leads, Deals, Companies, Contacts, etc.). Is this process easy?

Is there an option to use code (do you even want this - many businesses especially smaller ones won't) to create customizations to page views?

4. Integration with Other Applications. What does the CRM talk to? Can you use IFTTT or Zapier to create small automations between this CRM and other applications? Are there out of the box integrations and if so, what are they and do these integrations help your business?

5. Mobile App. Is mobile important to you? Most young sales people even if they are inside sales based may prefer to access CRM by mobile. Is there a mobile app? Do you need all

the same functions on the mobile app as the web based app? What features are available on a mobile device vs the web browser? Can you use a mobile responsive view on your smartphone i.e. still using a browser rather than downloading an iPhone or Android app?

6. Standard Objects and Fields. Think of "objects" as silos of data in CRM. They are categories of information. Common objects are Leads, Deals/Opportunities, Companies/Accounts, Contacts/People.

Inside of each of these objects there are data fields. What are the standard out of the box objects in the CRM you're looking at? Will you use these? What fields are out of the box? Do you need additional or different fields or labels for fields? (Usually this is 100% yes) If so what fields and going back to evaluation question #3, how easily can you add fields the business needs to augment Standard Fields. Can you add custom objects or are you limited to standard objects? Does this matter for what you need to accomplish?

7. Workflow Rules and Approvals. Some CRMs have no concept of built in workflow rules and approval tools. That might be fine. If you want to automate tasks, emails, call assignment, record assignment, etc., you may need this functionality. Is it a part of the CRM you're evaluating? If not, can you use a third-party party app like Zapier or IFTTT to accomplish this? Does this matter to you?

8. Team Selling, Roles-based Permissions. Can you create teams where information rolls up from reps to managers? How easy is it to control what type of users see what information? For example, can you make it so a sales rep sees only accounts and information they "own" in the CRM. But then, their boss or executives can see a consolidated roll-up of all reps on their team? Is this an important feature for you?

9. Administration. How do you control information? How do you determine roles for different types of users? Can you appoint an administrator using a role in the admin console of the CRM to control adding or suspending users? To control field or object security? What else can you do inside of an admin console? Can you control upload and download of data? How easy will it be for an admin to mass edit records? Are these features important to your business?

10. Cost per user. This always matters, let's not kid ourselves. What is the pricing model? Monthly per user fee? Annual? Old school software licensing? Do you need hardware, administration, hosting, bandwidth, storage? Are there limits to the volume of records you can store? Figuring out total costs and then understanding the true cost on average per user will be important when comparing options.

11. Calendar Integration. Most CRMs have some concept of a calendar or integration to a calendaring application. What does your company use? Google Calendar? Microsoft Outlook or Exchange? How does the CRM integrate with these? What are the features and

behaviors around adding new tasks or appointments? What is important to you and how would you like these two applications to work together?

12. Marketing Automation Options. Having CRM stand alone without the ability to communicate to other applications is a bad idea, generally. Specifically, there needs to be a source of truth on customer information and on prospects.

Part of your Marketing and Sales playbooks should define the hand off points and actions between these company functional groups. It should also describe ideally how information is created, acted upon and passes between systems. So, does the CRM you're evaluating talk to your marketing automation system? What is the nature of the synchronization of data. Is there the ability to report on information in each system or in a single system?

Defining the ideal scenario and comparing this to the actual functionality and interaction of these two critical systems is very important to choosing the right CRM and the correct marketing automation platform

13. Quotations Do your customers require quotations before they buy? How are you preparing quotes today? Rate that process in terms of the quality of quotes, the ease of creation, the ease of approvals, the accuracy in terms of product configuration and pricing. Then ask the approach to quotations that is available

to you using CRM. Is this a native function or is it a third-party add-on? Is it a feature add-on? How does the quotation process work? Is it a part of opportunity management? Is there even an option?

14. Is the CRM web based or does it require software installation? Listen, if you're confused on this, let's be clear. If the CRM you're evaluating is not Software as a Service, web hosted, run. Get very far away from it. This is not a debate. It's 2017 when I am writing this, not 1997. SaaS wins. Maybe this is ridiculous to a company that has a massive internal IT infrastructure, but Salesforce has proven this out. It's cheaper and easier and more scalable to operate this way. It's a secure method. Unless you're in the business of selling a CRM - why are you hosting the infrastructure of a CRM? There may be a case for on premise, but I think that is less and less the case. Rent your CRM seats, rent your marketing automation seats. Move on to other battles.

Web-Based Selling

Selling online needs to address two realities. The first is 85%+ of all purchases are now at least researched online before a buyer makes them. That says you need a strategy around content that addresses the buyer's journey. This falls to marketing generally. It can also, however, be important for sales to have a way to find and intercept buyers on social platforms, your website or blogs. The second reality is that when it comes to actually buying, some segments of business customers expect to be able to initiate a transaction themselves via an e-commerce web site.

While this can sometimes cut out salespeople per se, it also shapes the tasks and function of your sales team. Do you have a simple or complex product? If you have sales people in various functions discussed here- why? How can they contribute to an e-commerce type buyer education and sale? Do they even?

Web-based selling can incorporate your sales team. Connecting a live person with visitors to a website, e.g. using online messaging, social media monitoring and follow-up on new leads gathered from a website or landing page marketing opt in activity are all examples of where a real live human salesperson is part of the process of getting a prospect to become a customer in an e-commerce scenario.

Email communications become an important tool for both cold email outreach or nurturing type communications.

If I am selling business to consumer and have a simple product that can take the order without human interaction, I know as an entrepreneur that I need to provide some form of e-commerce transaction to my customer. The more complex the sale and the more complex the organization I am selling to (is this a B2B - business to business sale?) then I need to incorporate web based selling that may be a hybrid of sales team resources (humans) and automated digital tools.

The bigger the sale value, the more complex the buying process, the more complicated the organization - the more you need a human element. That doesn't 100% preclude the use of email automation, your website, social media, webinars, GoToMeeting/join.me type applications, e-signature technologies to sell better.

E-commerce

If my product can be purchased or consumed digitally, selling on my website, my mobile app or through an affiliate or my own website is important.

This probably falls to marketing and your technical lead to build, however, most of these sales processes could also involve human beings.

That being said, here is the decision matrix that you can use.

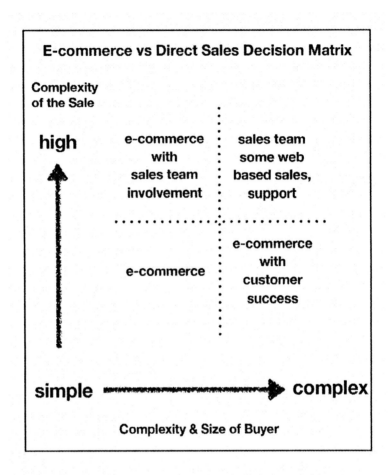

What Is a Sales Funnel?

While there certainly is a traditional sales funnel for direct sales representatives that consists of opportunities at different stages, this term has also come to be associated with e-commerce sales funnels. It may be more accurate to define this for e-commerce as the sales process that a prospect goes through before they buy and after. For example, you can see a common e-commerce sales funnel for a given customer - which really resembles the sales process of a direct sales rep.

Creating Automated E-commerce Sales Funnels

Before we dive into this list, we should briefly discuss some terms. We've <u>defined</u> sales funnels before, and even offer a handy <u>template</u>, but let's review what it is:

A sales funnel is "a series of steps designed to guide visitors toward a buying decision. The steps are composed of marketing assets that do the work of selling, like landing pages and email."

1. Example 1 – <u>CrazyEgg.com</u>
2. Example 2 – <u>Groupon.com's sales funnel</u>
3. Example 3 – <u>Grasshopper.com</u>

4. Example 4 – Basecamp
5. Example 5 – Mixergy.com
6. Example 6 – Planscope.io
7. Example 7 – AutoGrow
8. Example 8 – Harvest
9. Example 9 – Perfect Audience
10. Example 10 – Leadpages.net
11. Example 11 – HelpScout.com
12. Example 12 – Drift
13. Example 13 – Mint
14. Example 14 – Wufoo
15. Example 15 – MailChimp
16. Example 16 –
17. Example 17 – Netflix

Source: **https://autogrow.co/best-sales-funnel-examples/**

Landing Pages

A landing page is usually a standalone web page that is "contained". That is, you cannot navigate away from the offer on the page. The idea is to direct traffic to a page and have the prospect do something. If the promise of the email or advertisement was to get something free, often referred to as a lead magnet, e.g. free ebook, free report, free video, free checklist etc., then the landing page is where the prospects identify themselves in order to get the lead magnet.

That is, they see the offer in a video and text, they provide an email address and their name to go from anonymous to known. They are redirected to a page to download the lead magnet and sent an auto responder email.

201

Landing pages can also just direct the person to buy the product or service. I'm including this here because landing pages can be critical to both capture information and identify prospects. They can service as a way also to capture the actual sale. Again, this goes back to the complexity of your buyer and the complexity of the sale.

If you're in a more complex scenario and have decided to establish a sales team, marketing can set up lead magnets and landing pages that generate Lead records in your CRM and get assigned to sales people, usually Sales Development Representatives or Business Development Representatives.

These are clues for sales development reps to contact the newly identified person to find out more information about their needs, provide answers to questions and see if they are far enough along in their buying journey to warrant further assistance by the SDR, BDR, or, if appropriate, escalation to an Account Executive. AEs can help them with later stages of their buying journey. That is beyond qualification into more complex discovery, presentation, proposal, quotations and along the path through negotiations and closing a sale.

All of this from a landing page? Possibly. In the end, it is a tool but it is an important one that is often a bridge from marketing efforts into either a sale digitally or a sales engagement by a real live person.

Landing pages are often more of a feature of marketing automation platforms like Pardot, for example. Pardot allows marketers to generate landing pages that link to content.

They can also be a tool of BDRs doing outreach through email, social, LinkedIn selling or Account-

Based Sales. Whether your sales process is entirely automated, requires heavy human (sales team) involvement or is a hybrid, the Landing Page is in the mix.

Affiliates

Affiliates are independent digital sales partners. They send traffic to your offers. Usually you need to build an affiliate program and an Affiliate Manager to establish relationships with these partners and provide them a sales process, a digital sales funnel and materials that lead to a sale or lead that you pay them for.

Marketing Automation platforms like Infusionsoft offer a platform to manage affiliates and the programs that convert their traffic and transact sales for example.

Digital Sales Channels like App Stores

If you're selling mobile apps, you can consider iTunes and the Google Play store to be your sales channel. This requires more than you dropping an app on the store and hoping people find it.

Most likely you will have heavy marketing involvement.

There are good processes that define how to market and sell apps. This isn't necessarily the place for that, but know that mobile applications are a real channel. They can be a way to book customers into appointments, allow them to pay for goods and services. This can certainly be an extension of your e-commerce sales channel and even a way to build.

The Role of Email

Email remains an important tool for use by sales teams, whether one-off messages sent by reps using their individual email account or using their email identity through an automation tool like Mailchimp Pardot, Pardot Engage, reply.io or Salesloft for nurturing or cold email campaigns. HonchoCRM, for example, is a small business CRM that I am a partner in. The Honcho team are rolling out a sales outreach application that will allow sales teams to create outreach campaigns using stages email, phone calls or text messages to prospects or accounts. Similar tools are sold by Salesloft, Outreach.io, Yesware or Tout.

Sending automated notifications by email remains an important tool to use in your CRM. Any sort of workflow rule trigger or reassigning records might include an email notification for example. Other examples might be any updates to the status of support cases, the status of opportunities, orders or invoices being created.

Sales teams and automated sales funnels alike will still rely upon email as a way to communicate with customers. Text (SMS) messaging is increasingly being used in combination with email, however, it has not replaced this and likely will not.

Startup Metrics for Pirates

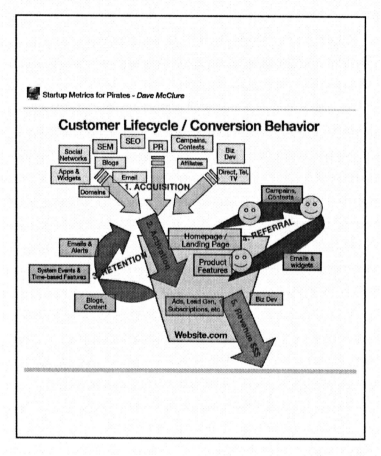

Dave McLure, the founder of 500 Startups, presented what I think is the clearest visual presentation of how to pull together a sales funnel, in his presentation titled Startup Metrics for Pirates. This title comes as a result of his acronym for Customer Lifecycle behavior for businesses that are mainly either an e-commerce or hybrid sales model, *AARRR* where the letters stand for *Acquisition, Activation, Retention, Referral and Revenue*. His example of the Customer Lifecycle/Conversion Behavior pulls together the elements of both a Traffic and Conversion

205

plan and the Sales Playbook. You will crea te your own model but this illustrates how an entire Automate and Grow program can work once implemented.

Expert Interview: Marko Brelih

Marko Brelih is a Marketing Consultant helping SME's and Sales Teams scale their business through the development of online sales processes and advertising. The main tools in his arsenal are FB advertising, inbound funnels, offer creation, marketing and sales automation and 'lethal copywriting.'

1. You specialize in creating online sales processes for businesses. What are 2-3 benefits of creating an automated sales process?

The old days of cold calling are almost officially dead. The real purpose of using digital sales processes is to

pre-sell, pre-screen and pre-qualify your leads and prospects. In doing so, you can:
a) Create awareness for your product/service and your unique brand
b) Identify and engage with hot leads, as well as,
c) Educate new entrants into your 'sphere of influence' about the solutions you can provide and establish yourself as both an authority and a person worth doing business with.

2. Does it matter what industry I am in? Can I leverage an online sales process?

It does not matter what industry you are in. Obviously, each scenario and business will require differing solutions depending on the norms of the industry, the price point of good/service sold, length of the sales cycle, and platforms where their current prospects/customers hang out.

For example, someone in a more traditional B2B space such as commercial real estate or finance may work more in authority building and engagement online, and bring the sales process to an offline call or meeting in the near future.

On the other end, someone selling coaching or virtual programs – whether it be personal development, executive, health or fitness – will look to leverage a shorter sales cycle and be more aggressive with the qualification of prospects and getting them to take action, perhaps conducting the sales process online via an automated webinar or Skype call.

That all being said, it has never been more important to establish an online presence and engage with prospects online as that is where most information is consumed and browsing/buying decisions are made.

3. If I am a start-up or even an existing small to medium sized business; what do I need to do before I dive into marketing automation?

Before businesses invest in systems to automate processes, they first need to establish a proof of concept with their offers and generate clients/sales. This means establishing their overall branding and positioning, fine tuning their sales process, and have some sort of organic marketing and lead generating/nurturing process. Once they move to scale lead gen and customer acquisition with paid advertising, they should look to automate these processes, so that they can focus on closing sales and servicing customers.

4. Outside consultant or full time marketing automation hire? In your mind, what makes more sense?

Great people are difficult to find. They often leave firms to start their own companies, are difficult to hire and train, and are expensive to keep. Ideally, you'll want to be in a position where you can afford to hire a rockstar and keep them.

That being said, it may be more realistic to find an outside consultant or agency that is crushing it in your given niche, or outsource everything to a Saas company and let them do the onboarding and management for you. They'll often be much more affordable, will provide a minimum of 2-3x ROI on your investment if they're established, and will have a much deeper understanding of the space if they work it full-time.

> 5. What do you think of Marketing committing to Service Level Agreements? e.g. generate a certain number of leads, quality of leads etc. over time that get passed along to a sales team?

When we try to control for certain goals or quotas, we may incentivize marketers or advertisers to go for 'cheap clicks.' Anyone can buy traffic and compile a large list of leads that isn't qualified or engaged. Marketers need to clearly convey the benefits of their products/services, and pre-sell, pre-screen and pre-qualify prospects so that the sales team can close easily. This process can take time, and so, I believe the focus should be on ensuring the quality of the marketing message and the core offering, without necessarily committing to hard goals.

Building a Direct Sales Model

Ok, so maybe e-commerce is not an entirely viable way to sell for your company on its own. Perhaps you realize you need a sales team trained in a sales process and managed correctly to outreach to prospects either identified by marketing, sales development activity or through some form of targeted account-based selling. How do you structure and set up this team?

Inside and Outside Sales Teams

If you're building a sales team, the trend generally is that you will want an inside sales team that is split along a few lines.

One is an inbound team that handles calls, emails and sales opportunities generated by marketing. Two is a proactive outbound sales group that is focused upon targeting accounts or buyers by email, LinkedIn prospecting and outbound telephone calling.

The final group could be considered either inside or outside sales. This is the Account Management team that handle sales opportunities once they are qualified by an inside group. Often, we have BDRs - Business Development Representatives and SDRs - Sales Development Representatives on the inside team. These either handle or generate new opportunities on a proactive basis. Once they qualify an account and confirm a potential sales opportunity, they hand it over to the Account Management team.

Inside sales has exploded, by the way. The cost benefits of an internal team that are both prospecting and closing deals has overtaken the traditional outbound sales team. With control over the sales process, companies can gain new prospects and business in a more predictable manner than ever before. Particularly this is true with inside sales teams where there is more consistency in automating the approach of each rep and the ability to provide managers on the spot feedback around approaches, tactics and customer tendencies. Inside sales for many organizations has become a lab and a science unto itself on customer acquisition and product effectiveness.

Sales environments are shifting and <u>inside sales is growing three times faster than traditional sales.</u> If you're just getting started or looking to grow and scale your inside sales team, you need a <u>uniform playbook</u> each of your sales reps can follow.

This is unlike the more variable approach of traditional outbound sales people that might be traveling, communicating in different manners, delivering different messages, and in different manners.

Understanding what an inside vs outside team's focus needs to be is critical to gaining success using either or both in some combination.

An amazing resource in deciding how to build both is the book *Predictable Revenue* by Aaron Ross and Mary Lou Tyler. Aaron's claim to fame is that he built the first outbound sales team at Salesforce.com. This has been referred to by Inc Magazine as the Sales Bible of Silicon Valley. In it, I think he correctly evangelizes that roles in a sales team need to be distinct and focused upon one segment of the sales process. Here are some common roles that fall into these categories.

Business Development Representatives

This role today is largely around research and having many touches with a client before they are ready to buy.

While marketing can play a role in identifying and warming up prospects, a BDR is usually a role that targets a group of accounts (Account-Based Selling) and finds the right contacts within these accounts and engages them in a conversation to help figure out if they are in an active buying process, get them ready to buy or help them make choices while they are trying to buy.

Sales Development Representatives

The definition of a sales development rep (SDR) is a type of inside sales rep that solely focuses on outbound prospecting. Many companies (such as Salesforce) have experienced massive revenue growth by separating sales organizations into specific roles.

Account Executives

Closers. These are the experts, the relationship managers. Account Executives are focused on dealing with the gritty details that bring a customer from merely being qualified deeper into the buying process.

This is the team member who makes presentations to prospective customers, including explaining your company's capabilities. AEs ask the right questions to understand detailed customer needs, buying processes and roles.

Account Executives are also responsible for preparing and providing accurate proposals and quotes to the customer.

Account Executives will discover and address alternatives the client might be evaluating. They will take the lead on negotiation of terms and conditions on the way to a final contract or agreement.

They will also need to be savvy enough to understand when subject matter experts like Sales Engineers or Service Delivery Managers need to be brought in to present to the customer. They paint the picture on how life will look day to day after the customer buys.

These resources are closers and experts on complex sales. This includes discovery of client needs, presenting capabilities of the company and options, providing quotations and proposals, negotiation of terms and contracts, and losing the sale with the client.

Director of Sales

Directly manages 5-20 BDRs, SDRs. Gets involved in opportunities and helps coach his team to advance sales opportunities. Needs information on sales funnels and deals and makes sure there is the right culture of accountability, fun and excellence.

These guys can be a total nightmare as the organization drops demands on them around reporting and funnels and forecasting. A lot of companies really screw this role up these days. If you want a high-performing sales culture, don't just treat these guys like information hawks because that will 100% trickle down and turn into games. Hire leaders not managers.

Vice President of Sales

The VP of Sales picks a great team that includes hiring Directors of Sales. They create a framework where there are succession plans, team leaders. They are responsible for creating a great sales culture. The VP of Sales helps communicate to his senior leadership counterparts how things are moving forward.

Sales forecasting has become a beast in bigger companies.

213

Everyone who is left brained wants a crystal ball. We need discipline but relationships matter too. Being experts matters. Communicating product and service delivery needs matters. Sales sometimes wants a magic product, sometimes they have valid market feedback. VPs need to sift through this and convey strategic information to product marketing, marketing, and customer support about what is happening in sales conversations with prospects and customers. What do customers like, dislike, need, want and what will they spend money on?

Tools used by Sales Teams

While CRM remains the central place for customer data whether you have an automated sales funnel, e-commerce or you have a direct sales team, there are other web-based tools that have become important to consider. With the growth of inside sales, there is the growth of digital selling tools. Some of the more popular ones include:

- WebEx, Join.me and other remote meeting, conferencing and presentation tools.
- Esignature tools to gain digital contract sign off, like DocuSign, Adobe Sign, PandaDoc.
- Quote to Cash or CPQ (Configure Price Quote). This is a category of software like Steelbrick from Salesforce or Apptus that allows you to empower sales reps to assemble quotes that look great, match product, pricing business rules, get internal and customer sign off and more.
- Zapier or IFTTT are web-based services where an end user can integrate the web applications they use. For example, need to create a simple automation between Salesforce and a Google Spreadsheet? Maybe you want to

create a new Invoice in QuickBooks whenever you have a new order in your CRM. These are all examples of simple integrations that these types of platforms allow a non-technical team member (e.g. sales, marketing) to create.

- Box.com, Dropbox or Google Drive - this has become an easy and important category of tools for sales reps. This becomes an option to consider when thinking about how to store and share documents, presentations, proposals, digital brochures, contracts or agreements, for example, with customers.

Indirect Sales Channels

Indirect channels are basically third-party partners who you support and sell through. This can include Value-Added Resellers, Integration Partners, Distributors or other partners who take your product, service or software and either sell it to their customer base, or offer a component, service or software to your base that you do not want to offer directly.

Third Party Sales

If your business sells products, service or software through agents, resellers or other third-party sellers, there are many things you can look at automating, including:

- Partner Communities
- Partner Forums
- Partner Knowledge
- Channel Marketing Support
- On-boarding
- Sales Assets and tools

- Channel sales funnels
- Ordering and Fulfillment
- Tier 2 and 3 level support models

Retail

Similarly, if you sell through retail, you likely have to support retailers by stocking shelves, facilitating orders, providing in store point of sale. Retail is crumbling under the weight of e-commerce, and specifically Amazon—btw this is potentially a sales channel you need to consider, however, there are businesses that need to support retail partners.

Again, whether via your website or a partner community, there are many of the same opportunities to digitally support sales, ordering, fulfillment, shelve restocking, etc. for retail partners and channels.

Partners

By partners, we mean many things, but this could include, but not be limited to:

- Software Development partners
- Alliance partners
- Referral Partners
- Integration Partners
- Value-Added Resellers

Whether it is publishing a development kit (SDK) or API for software partners to plug into parts of your data that can attract additional business, extend your products, services, data, applications through the applications built by partners. Or perhaps your software needs external partners to customize or integrate it,e.g. Salesforce has a partner model, Apple has partner models for iPhone app development, and Mac app development.

Perhaps your business lends itself to its own app store to highlight third-party apps that work with your software, products or services.

Bluetooth SIG, for example, the special interest group that sets Bluetooth standards, has various partners that either use their technology to design, build radio devices, incorporate the radios into products - for example, how about that combination water bottle + Bluetooth speaker you saw at Walmart the other day, hmmm?

Whether you have a partner program or you decide to create one, this becomes a way to sell more (read: GROWTH) and to support partners using automation websites, communities, and portals as an example.

Expert Interview: Aaron Symbolik

For insights on the current state of selling, I turn to Aaron Symbolik. Aaron is a seasoned sales management professional with over 14 years of success in the payroll industry.

Aaron has been successful in building and managing sales teams as well as being a sales professional.

As a manager, his teams consistently exceed quotas, achieving 140-200% of targets and has lead the top performing sales team in the country for Paylocity.

He is also an expert on using CRM, Marketing Automation and Business Development tactics to grow and close sales opportunities.

MD: How Important is creating a Sales Playbook for your teams and managing against a defined sales process?

Aaron Symbolik: Sales success always should be measured to a process that can produce predictable outcomes. Of course, the playbook will vary by industry and market trends and is constantly evolving.

I always said that sales is like a game of blackjack. Under the right conditions on the table, when you play the game by a specific set of rules, it will have more predictable outcomes in which instead of taking a 7-8% loss, you will beat the house by 0.5%. In sales, you win some and lose some.

You either lose a sale to status quo or you lose to a competitor. If you have a playbook that has been developed and proven in the field, you can deploy that playbook and constantly measure results across your sales force.

Undoubtedly, when you start to analyze the losses, you will find many times key steps are missed in the process and many excuses of why those steps were skipped seem to follow.

So, a playbook provides structure and a framework by which you can measure your company's success and the success of your sales teams.

Other than following a set of rules for predictable outcomes, the playbook should set the sales rep up for success, lending them credibility. Does your playbook educate potential buyers on industry trends from leading experts? Does your playbook not only look to address current needs but does it bring a unique perspective to get businesses to think differently about their business?

It starts to now become about the needs a prospective client may have five years from now. So, the playbook lends credibility to the sales rep's pitch to bring actual value to the conversation. A part of the playbook is getting a passive buyer to an active buying state or even an active buyer to accept an evaluation criterion. In service and technology most companies don't have a formal buying process.

Recently, Gartner Consulting put out what is regarded as the most comprehensive white paper on doing these evaluations.

The six criteria are Vendor Vision (does your company's vision match up to our customers?), Vendor Viability (what revenue do they invest back into their technology?), Technical Architecture and Integrations (do they have a modern platform that is an open platform that plays well with other applications through the use of APIs?), Product Functionality (does the user experience keep up with today's technology and methodology?), Service Quality, and Investment.

219

Lastly and most importantly, a company's "why" or vision and purpose becomes a big role. This was outlined by Simon Sinek, author of *Start with Why*. Sinek said that companies don't buy from you because of how or what you do, but they buy because of why you do what you do and is perfectly aligned with the physiology of the brain when making emotional decisions.

MD: How do sales teams leverage the internet today when considering the impact of buyers doing research on the internet the past 5-7 years?

Aaron Symbolik: I think marketing in general has leveraged SEO in retail and b2b to drive better traffic and buying habits for consumers.

In Business to Business sales, the internet becomes important to the individual sales rep in researching market trends, organizational changes within companies, identifying key stakeholders, and researching competitors.

YouTube has played a large role as well when researching any sort of technology looking for competitive advantages.

MD: What do you think are the critical sales automation tools today?

Aaron Symbolik: Marketing and Sales automation many people feel are one and the same, but they are, for sure, two different animals.

The definition of sales automation is simply having technology work on your behalf while you sleep or perform other tasks. CRM automation for task reminders, automated drip campaigns that provide relevant articles to potential future customers have been mission critical.

They say that follow up, or lack of, is the death of a salesperson. Considering the speed at which technology is advancing and evolving, it's becoming a necessity to leverage these tools.

One thing I have noticed is that with the onset of millennials and especially younger millennials, they feel much more comfortable using technology to perform and keep them on task.

You have to think how millennials grew up. They grew up around the internet. Generation Z right behind them grew up in the internet. Fifteen years ago, phone calls were always the preferred method for contacting prospective clients for critical conversations like price negotiations and setting next steps.

Millennials seem perfectly comfortable using email for these critical conversations, although doing so with generations before them could hurt their sale. But this may be perfectly OK when communicating with other millennials.

Examples of sales automation is email marketing apps such as HonchoEmail, Marketo, and Constant Contact. Tools like CRM can automate suggested tasks based on an activity with accounts and remind you when you should be following up with important prospects.

MD: If you were dropped into a start-up today, how would you structure the roles on your sales team?

Aaron Symbolik: You have to consider who your audience is. A product or service can be strictly sold on the internet through Search Engine Optimization and pay per click campaigns and driving traffic to your product.

You can use an inside sales force to sell anywhere in the world, or you can hire an outside sales force that presents in person, or really a combination of any or all of these. The other trend in selling technology is utilizing a technical or functional expert to demonstrate technology while the sales individual drives the sales process and controls the key stakeholders.

Salesforce is an example of technology sold in this fashion. There has been a trend recently where selling tech in this way is being done remotely through tools like zoom or GoToMeeting. There are pros and cons, of course. One of the critical cons of not being present with a potential customer is that you cannot read nonverbal responses and cues if you're not in the room.

Humans will display so many of these during a demonstration preventing sales from identifying points in the presentation to stop and discuss. If, for example, I showed something and the prospect got visually excited but said nothing, how would I expand on what she liked about that particular feature or function?

As a company starts off small, it may just start with a couple sales individuals managed by the CEO. Then, as they grow, there becomes a need for a larger ladder and a hierarchy for sales management.

So, you might have a sales manager and a team below them. As you expand further from that, you may have a V.P. of Sales that leads several Regional managers directly responsible for other sales managers managing sales reps. It becomes necessary to grow in this fashion for obvious reasons.

One person can only manage so much. Depending on your product, you may have a need to approach your startup with a seasoned sales professional and a technical expert.

Whether they sell this way or remote or one is remote and the other is on site, it does not matter. Each of you have a role and it's clear to the prospect which one of you is an expert in which area.

If they need to lean on someone to guide them through a difficult evaluation, that responsibility will fall on the sales rep. If there is a function they want to explore further to make sure it meets some sort of gap, then they can lean on the functional expert. You now have a functional sales team.

MD: You've mainly worked in business to business sales environments. How do you decide the level of selling through digital vs sales rep supported efforts?

Aaron Symbolik: I think it really depends on the complexity of the product. If it's a simple product that is unique but pretty straightforward, you may want to consider on-line only or a combination of on-line and inside sales.

Many CRM tools are sold this way today. As the product and functions become more complex and it feels more natural meeting with a buying team, then in person is the way to go.

The other consideration is product differentiation and competitors. Are you selling a commodity or do you have a unique perspective? If your competitors are meeting with your prospect in person and you're meeting remotely, you're missing out on quality rapport building.

There is an old adage that people buy from who they like. Actually, this is not true. People will still buy from people they don't like. People will buy from who provided the most credibility and value. It just so happens being in person can play favorably in building credibility and value as things are conveyed much differently this way.

Chapter Summary Points

1. It is important that your business create a written Sales Playbook to articulate your approach to customers.
2. Part of this will be to define not only key messages, but also sales process, sales team roles and responsibilities.
3. This should also define whether your sales model is digital (e-commerce), via a direct sales team or a hybrid of the two.
4. The use of Customer Relationship Management software (CRM) is critical to be the brain of your sales, marketing and support automations. This information will bridge all three functions. It also serves as the basis of providing an awesome Customer Experience and automating workflows, processes, approvals and task handoff and assignment between teams and team members.

References

https://www.marketo.com/resources/marketing-and-sales-alignment/
https://blog.omniconvert.com/e-commerce-funnel.html
https://autogrow.co/best-sales-funnel-examples/
https://quickbooks.intuit.com/r/marketing/how-to-create-an-e-commerce-sales-funnel/
https://www.metrilo.com/blog/ecommerce-conversion-funnels-practical-guide/
https://www.slideshare.net/dmc500hats/startup-metrics-for-pirates-long-version/2-Customer_Lifecycle_5_Steps_to
https://hbr.org/2012/07/the-end-of-solution-sales
http://www.nimble.com/blog/writing-a-killer-sales-playbook/
http://www.ringdna.com/blog/5-killer-sales-playbook-examples
https://blog.hubspot.com/sales/sales-process-cheat-sheet-template
https://hbr.org/2012/08/the-new-sales-playbook
http://labs.openviewpartners.com/sales-playbook/#.WZKpO9PyvOQ
https://www.demandmetric.com/content/sales-playbook-template
http://events.bulldogsolutions.com/KnowledgeBase/SalesPlaybookBD.pdf
https://www.marketo.com/ebooks/sales-playbook-essentials-in-brief/
http://info.qvidian.com/rs/qvidian/images/howtocreateakillersalesplaybook.pdf
https://www.slideshare.net/revegy/webinar-using-sales-playbooks-that-align-with-the-buyers-journey

For more about competitive analysis: Think Like the Competition

Chapter 7: Post Sales Customer Interaction: Support, Service, and Success

Large companies have figured out that the most expensive interaction post sales is between a customer and a customer service representative.

Most small and medium-sized businesses consider customer support an expensive luxury.

For sure, it can be a slow, painful process for a customer calling into a call center - the traditional support scenario we all envision where the call center's entire goal is to "resolve" your problem as quickly and cheaply as humanly possible. Not the best experience.

Furthermore, this elicits visions of talking to someone in a far-off land with limited verbal, reasoning or decision-making skills.

When done wrong, customer support is little more than a pass the buck exercise by a customer support agent.

When done correctly however, that call gets routed to the correct resource, who has answers and makes your customer experience a positive one.

More importantly, the traditional telephone call never occurs. Instead, customer issues and questions are resolved without human interaction, freeing up customer support to become "customer success" or "customer joy" focused individuals who retain or derive new opportunity and revenue for your business.

Cost of Acquiring a Customer

Getting a new customer is an expensive process these days. The effort between marketing and sales is not insignificant as we have details. It goes to reason that once you have acquired a customer, your goal should be to sell them something again and then... again. Keep them happy, use them as a reference. Leverage that acquisition.

For very small companies, the goal becomes paramount, but also a little daunting. Are you investing tons of time into a customer without incremental revenue or new opportunity? Are you set up so that post sales interactions pay off? The problem is customer support for all of us seems like an expensive luxury we cannot provide.

The ultimate answer for those of us in the small to medium-sized business space is to provide support resources, a path of support that is self-service as much as possible. This is what large companies have discovered.

It goes to reason that you can implement some support resources for customers even if you are a very small company.

Case Management

If you do have an inquiry or question from a client, how do you manage it?

Any sort of post-sales customer request or inquiry should be logged somewhere in a software system and managed as a "case".

A Case is a record in your CRM or trouble ticketing system of how and when a customer contacted you, the nature of their problem, the status and resolution of the case.

Ideally, web-based resources should be the first line of defense allowing a customer to resolve their own question or problem. If not, we use a case record - in the end this needs to be recorded under the Account in CRM, to route, notify and track the resolution of the inquiry.

Case management can be a feature of your CRM. It can also be an external application like Zendesk, FreshDesk, Salesforce Service Cloud, Jira Service Desk, etc., that is used by customer support agents to manage cases. If you decide to use a case management system external to CRM, the case should still be recorded in CRM. In the end, the source of truth on all customer interactions pre-sales, during an opportunity, or post sales should somehow end up in CRM.

How Do Cases Get Initiated?

How can customers contact you and let you know they have a question or problem they need help with? There are 5-6 common ways this can occur.

Web Self Service

Your website may be the greatest source of information for new customers, but what about existing customers?

Start with some basics. Do you have a list of FAQs (frequently asked questions) for existing customers? Adding a Customer Support section on your website and promoting this to existing customers will go a long way.

What are the common questions or problems that customers call you about? Are there 'how to' descriptions for your product, service or software? No? Add them!

YouTube Videos

The best way to help your customers post sales might be to record a series of YouTube videos on common questions and problems and to provide this as a library to clients. This, when done right, is a done once, used forever type resource. It provides visual demonstration of common problem resolution and a video feels very personal compared to a written FAQ and is less open to interpretation by the customer.

Knowledge Base

A knowledge base is really a searchable directory of Questions and Answers. This can be something you build into your website.

Depending on whether you have an actual customer support organization, it is also a common feature of many customer support applications that can be used internally by support reps, but also extended out to customers via website or web portal.

Questions are typically the inquires or problems that customers have. They can also be issues Support reps encounter.

229

Answers can be the best resolution used by support representatives.

Community-Based Support

If you are smaller, a Questions and Answer Knowledge base can often also be a community-based system where customers post Questions and other Customers in the community post solutions and vote up the best responses. Your support reps can participate in community discussions and provide the "official" company answer.

Social Media-Based Support

Does your company have a Twitter or Facebook profile? Often, customers will comment or message for support via these channels. Twitter, in particular, can be a good place to direct support. For example, maybe you create a specific Twitter ID that is your support Twitter account.

Telephone-Based Support

The old school call center. These are the single most expensive and sometime ineffective calls in the universe. Most companies recognize this and create so many other paths to support BEFORE a phone call is initiated.

Your goal should be to make these interactions amazing.... and infrequent. Creating all the other lines of support gives anyone actually taking a 1:1 support phone call an arsenal of answers and tools to also redirect clients to.

The actual support interaction, however, should become very managed. Not automated, we want to be personal, but consistent and supported by the same tools we are describing here.

Email to Case

Customers should be able to initiate an email based case. This allows them to send an email that generates a case record in your CRM or Trouble Ticketing system. Then responses can be in writing and therefore documented and point to resources like Knowledge base articles, guides, YouTube videos, etc.

Web to Case

Clients should be able to initiate a support case (inquiry, problem, etc.) via a web-based form that creates an open case in your CRM or trouble ticketing system. Typically, this includes them providing an email address and phone number. This will, ideally, in CRM match up with an existing Account so there is a reference to what products or services they have with you, and what role the inquirer fulfills.

Chat-Based Support

Another type of support that is personal is web-based Chat. You want to also try to have a chat solution that will record the interaction in CRM (see a theme here?).

Chat is very inexpensive compared to telephone-based support. Typically, a single support rep can handle 4-5x more cases via chat than a telephone-based response. Also, you have more visual tools, including links to articles, videos and other knowledge resources that are more difficult to provide for telephone-based agents.

Customer Success vs Customer Support

The concept of Customer Success particularly applies to businesses with recurring revenue models where there is an ongoing revenue stream and thus motivation to keep customers happy and on the platform or service. This also becomes a cultural mantra for Automate and Grow businesses where instead of trying to resolve issues, customer interactions are seen as a part of the Customer Journey.

Idea Shift: The Customer Success Team

The concept of Customer Success is one which is relatively new. You may see customer success managers as a role at companies, particularly SaaS or services-based companies that you deal with. I asked out loud when I first saw this sort of title, 'Sounds cool, is that just a fancy title for a customer service representative?"

When I researched it, I found that this is a new model of retaining customers.

The key difference to start seems to be that, philosophically, Customer Service is reactive and Customer Success is proactive. Customer Success methodologies try to proactively have people from your company post sales connect with clients in an automated fashion. Customer Success teams engage customers.

1.	They are calling to get the customer to use the product/service/application they bought;
2.	Provide new ideas or offers;

3.   Up-sell with new features that might help the client;

4.   Retain customers by getting feedback and providing a clear path to answers and problem resolution before they fester or arise.

> "(Customer Success) It's a proactive, real-time sales approach consisting of building relationships with existing customers, understanding in depth their company and product goals, and helping the customer meet those goals through day-to-day contact. Each customer has different needs and uses for your product, so it's up to the Customer Success Manager (CSM) to thoroughly understand each customer and to be their champion throughout their entire customer journey. The role of the CSM is a value-add and is usually not a fee-based service."

> Source: Client Success: Customer Success vs Customer Support

The Cost of Loss

The concept of churn is born out of businesses that have a recurring revenue model. For example, service providers, Software as a Service subscription-based businesses all live by the accumulation of built-in recurring business. These businesses grow exponentially, and you will hopefully be building these products and services into your revenue mix.

The reality is that if a customer has a cost of acquisition, the return on that acquired customer takes time to realize. For example, in my olden days of working for cellular phone carriers, we had a known cost of acquisition between marketing, sales and subsidizing the customer to get on the network (read: cell phone cost subsidies).

Then we knew based upon the revenue plan of the customer that it would take xx months (let's call this 7 months) to break even on that upfront cost to our business.

In the cellular industry a customer was generally locked into a contract, so we knew that less the costs of capital and operating costs on average the customer was profitable from month 8-24.

Churn was our calculation of the number of foundational, base customers that would leave for a competitor. Software as a Service, recurring revenue, and subscription-based businesses also feel this churn pain.

If you do not control churn, you will not grow exponentially, you will shrink! Ouch. If 1% vs 1.5% of your customer base churns a month, what's the big deal as long as you are adding new customers? That's 50% different monthly but annually, we're talking cumulative much larger numbers. If your base grows, the absolute number grows too as a percentage. Here's a chart to illustrate. Just know that if you're churning 1.5% of your customer base a month, you're losing 20%+ per year.

Sample Calculation:

For example, if Company ADG had $500,000 MRR at the beginning of the month, $450,000 MRR at the end of the month, and $65,000 MRR in upgrades that month from existing customers, its revenue churn rate would be:

Revenue Churn Rate =
[(MRR beginning of month – MRR end of month) – MRR in upgrades during month] / MRR beginning of month
(($500,000 – $450,000) – $65,000)/$500,000 =
($50,000 – $65,000)/$500,000 =
(-$15,000)/$500,000 = -3%
Source: Evergage, Inc.: How to Calculate Customer Churn

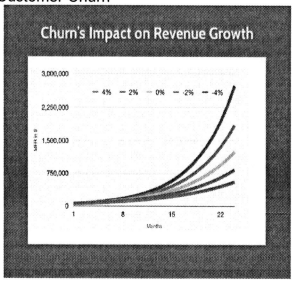

Source: Chargify: SaaS Customer Success

Below is a model of a Customer Success Journey might look like:

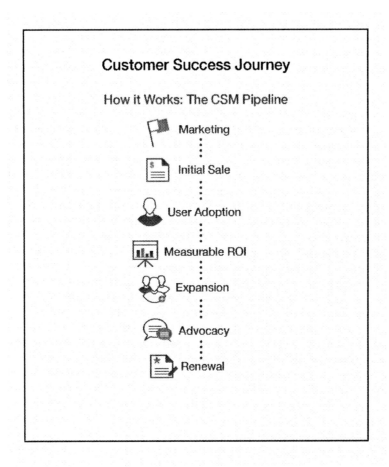

Source: Chargify: SaaS Customer Success

1. **Customer Development**: Before a sales pitch is ever delivered, the CS team learns about the customer and what her unique needs are.

2. **Customer Pitch**: Once the company has a good idea about what the customer's needs are, the sales pitch is made and the customer is shown how and why a particular product or service will benefit and enhance his needs.

3. **Acquisition**: If the case has been adequately made as to the benefit of a service

or product, the customer will commit to complete the purchase.

4. **Onboarding**: During this process, you'll be working out all the details and logistics of getting your customer to switch to your product or service. There is sometimes a technical component to this process, and this is where your customer service team plays an important part.

5. **Staying Engaged**: Now that the sale has been made and your customer converted, the role of the CSM continues. Staying engaged with the customer and regularly checking in to make sure the product or service is functioning as intended is important.

6. **Customer Service**: As you customer uses your product, she may have issues or questions that arise and will need to access your customer service team.

7. **Continuing Engagement**: Over time, your customer's needs may change and by staying engaged, you'll be able to respond and grow with her. (This is where the ROI on a CS team is realized!)

Introducing the Customer Success Manager

A Customer Success Manager should be:

1. looking at ways to improve user on-boarding (via data and user feedback);

2. looking at data to identify red flag metrics that indicate accounts are at risk of churning;

3. proactively reaching out to those at-risk accounts to re-engage them;

4. identifying accounts who could benefit from an upsell/upgrade (perhaps the customer is currently paying overage fees and a better solution is to upgrade to the next plan) and proactively reaching out to them to facilitate the upgrade.

Customer Support

What is customer support or service? While Customer service is about account-based issues, e.g. billing, features, Customer support is truly its own function. This group, which seeks to solve individual product issues or provide product guidance for specific customers, is often more reactive in nature as the customer is usually calling to report a ticket or a problem they are encountering. Often, B2B SaaS businesses have varying levels of service offerings and usually operate on a fee-for-service model.

This might be one contracted resource offshore or a team dedicated to connecting with customers to figure out how things are going, what more you can provide them. In the end, it's about keeping customers you have spent time and money to acquire. This should not be salespeople, marketing or executives. This team may incorporate any of the above, but really it needs to be a distinct role with clear objectives to make sure customers stay, spend the same or more.

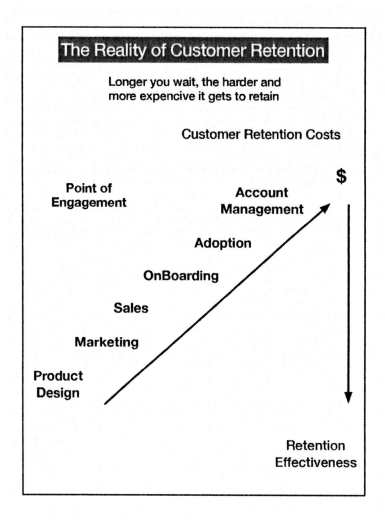

Source: Customer Success Association, Michael Blasidell and Associates.

Automated Outreach

An important key to providing automated self-service customer support will be communicating with your clients that something is done. What are the common communications that your customer would like to receive by email? By text? What event triggers this communication?

Automate this so it happens every time. Is a new account setup? Has a new case been logged? Has someone replied to a case? Is the status of the case changed from opened to in progress or to closed? Do you require a reply from the customer? Think these steps through and create triggers and actions in your support process that handle these so they happen every time.

Up-Selling

How can you increase the services or products your customer has from you? A well resolved case should lead to a new offer that is automated. What software, services products or features can you offer to your customers at the point of support?

Human Contact Point

What people are on your customer success team? What is their expertise? At what point should they come in contact with a client?

Think about the common problems that can be best resolved by a human being and what the ideal resolutions are. Build these into a process and automate it using workflow rules, triggers, knowledge articles.

What culture do you want to create in this success group? What role do they play in your providing an awesome customer experience? How are they paid? What image do you want them to portray? Should they be easy to deal with or difficult?

How will you measure success?

There are some common ways a success team should be measured:

1. Churn Rate
2. Monthly Recurring Revenue (MRR)
3. Committed Monthly Recurring Revenue (CMRR)
4. Cash
5. Customer Acquisition Cost (CAC)
6. Customer Lifetime Value (CLTV)
7. Net Promoter Score (NPS) or other customer loyalty measures
8. Customer Satisfaction Measures
9. Quantitative assessments of the primary emotions your customers are experiencing at specific stages or touchpoints in their journey
10. Measures of effort
11. Measures of importance, helpfulness, etc. of a specific touchpoint

Getting Feedback

What feedback mechanisms from customer to success team member should be in place? Often, companies will automate follow-up after a sale or during the customer life cycle using surveys. Customer satisfaction surveys focus on measuring customer perceptions of how well a company delivers on the critical success factors and dimensions of the business.

Setting criteria for scoring these interactions can be used as triggers in your trouble ticketing or case management system for proactive outreach to at risk customers. Tracking the Sat Score can be an important metric particularly for SaaS or subscription-based businesses.

Using technology to lighten the load on customers and internal resources

1. Website FAQ
2. YouTube channel
3. Customer Forum or Community
4. Customer Portal
5. Support/Success Blog Articles
6. Knowledge Database of problems & resolutions

Expert Interview: Greg Meyer

When I want to know the real dope on building out technology and capabilities in the customer service, support and success arenas, I ask one person: Greg Meyer. Greg has worked for some interesting companies, including most recently Kustomer -- a Customer Experience SaaS startup out of New York. He's also worked at building customer support/success teams and systems at Blackberry, Salesforce, Rival IQ and Pro.com.

I asked Greg a few questions to get to the heart of building out a great customer service and success function in your business. This includes the technology needed to empower customers and team members.

MD: You have worked as an expert or leader in a number of notable companies around the customer service function including Salesforce, Blackberry and now Kustomer. How do business leaders view Customer Service in general today as a business function? Necessary evil or Opportunity for Customer Engagement?

Greg Myer: Customer service today is having a crisis. More than ever before, customers have increasing expectations for brands (based on their experience with consumer software platforms) and those brands don't meet their needs. The brands are trying hard and have changed the way they do business, but there is still a gap between customers and brands in terms of the customer experience.

Brands that recognize this issue and are trying to fix it realize that customer service data is integral to the rest of their business.

These brands are using automation to identify areas where they can improve their business process and using that extra time to deliver more personalized service to their customers. With that knowledge, they are developing valuable intelligence to help them predict customer behavior and future experiences.

MD: What is the role of technology today for companies and their c/s leaders?

Greg Myer: The role of technology today is to remove barriers between companies and their customers and identify what customers really want and need. Technology is not a silver bullet - it is a way to coordinate the people, process, and tools that need to be in place to deliver great support - and often it is not only the tools that need to change but also the underlying business process.

MD: What do you think the biggest barrier to adopting these technologies is for companies?

Greg Myer: The biggest barrier to adopting new tools for companies is "we've done it this way for a long time and it works OK." Inertia is a powerful barrier to identifying the change that needs to take place first to quantify the benefits of change and then to create process and execution to drive that change.

MD: The concept of a call center makes most actual customers cringe I think as a means of support. What are the important channels today other than telephone call centers?

Greg Myer: Customers care about being contacted quickly and accurately in their channel of choice. They don't really care whether the contact happens in a call center as long as they are treated well, get their question answered to their satisfaction, and don't have to ask to solve the same question again.

MD: I see roles in more and more companies today with the term 'Customer Success.' Is this just code for

Customer Service or is there something else culturally different going on here?

Greg Myer: There is something completely different going on when companies create a customer success function. Customer success - typically used in subscription businesses - is focused on creating the conditions for account success and expansion. Customer service is reactive and focused on solving problems, and less on creating fewer opportunities to need support.

MD: What would you say are the 2-3 most important things a company should address when looking at ways to Automate Customer Support?

Greg Myer:

- Identify the 5-10 most frequently occurring problems you have
- Brainstorm 3 things you could do to solve these
- Identify the best 5-10 items to automate based on the frequency of the item, the cost of handling that issue, and the cost of getting it wrong

MD: What are a few ways an effective Customer Success team helps a company grow in your opinion?

Greg Myer: Identify the characteristics of successful customers and the key things those customers get done in their first 7, 30, and 90 days as customers. Ask customers and prospects about the thing they think is easiest and is hardest with your software or product or service. Interview customers who decide to stop buying your product or service and ask them about the one thing you could have done to keep them. If they answer "nothing," ask them what they would do to help another customer in their situation.

Chapter Summary Points

1. Creating a Customer Journey Roadmap will help you define how you will support customers using multiple channels, such as phone, email, web, social or chat.
2. This will then provide a framework for implementing Customer Experience technology like Salesforce Service Cloud or Zen Desk to manage customer cases.
3. The concept Customer Success is a proactive approach to consider as opposed to traditional 'support' or 'service' models which are reactive.
4. Being proactive is critical today, particularly for software as a service businesses where customer happiness is critical to growing revenue over time.

References

http://www.customersuccessassociation.com/definition-customer-success-management/

https://www.clientsuccess.com/blog/customer-success-vs-customer-support/

http://www.evergage.com/blog/how-calculate-customer-churn-and-revenue-churn/

https://www.chargify.com/blog/saas-customer-success/

Chapter 8: Your Automate and Grow Dream Team

Once you have created your Automate and Grow plan, you will need to assemble a team of resources both internal and external to build the applications, processes and ultimately chart your business.

There are basically five categories of team members

1. Internal employees
2. Contractors, freelancers, consultants
3. Agencies & Service Providers
4. Channel Partners
5. Customers or Clients

Examples of Team Resources you need on your Automate and Grow Development and Implementation Project

Project Leader: The *Project Leader* will serve as your team's primary point of contact. Project Leaders are responsible for ensuring the development process is executed correctly to maximize benefit and facilitate the successful delivery of your project. The Project Leader will be responsible for tracking and reporting on solution progress and project status. In owning the execution of the development and implementation process, the Project Leader will also be responsible for supporting the Product Owner in his or her understanding of the process and expectations.

Software Consultant: A Consultant is a platform expert (for example this could be a Salesforce Consultant, a CRM Consultant etc.) with technical understanding of Salesforce Sales, Service and Pardot Marketing Clouds. The Sr. Consultant also provides subject matter expertise around business, sales,

247

service and marketing automation. They are typically interfacing with various company stakeholders (internal and external) to design a vision, strategy and plan that serves as the overarching success map for your Salesforce implementation. They can contribute to business goals by understanding and advising clients of best practices, new ideas and strategies to grow sales, improve sales effectiveness, transform business through automation, grow leads and opportunities through marketing automation and/or by growing customer sales, margins and satisfaction through customer service and support strategies. They will also have an understanding of technical solutions including those enabled by third party solutions.

Software Developer(s): Software Developers are trained and capable software development resources who can customize the CRM, web, case management or marketing automation platform through a combination of object and field creations, security and permission setup, user setup, integration of data into the system, custom page views based upon user roles. They are generally familiar with a specific software application or platform including platform capabilities and limitations. They work with and around these to implement the best software solutions to meet business requirements.

Project Manager: A Project Manager is responsible for keeping the team organized and on track. They work to ensure that requirements are understood and clearly communicated and that developers are working towards feature and solution implementations that support the overall project goals and deliverables.

Software Architect: The *Technical Architect* is a member of the Development team and is responsible for the vision and ultimate technical design of any integration or application development needs. The

Technical Architect is responsible for technology selection and development methodology that may be required during your project. This role can both deliver and govern the execution of development deliverables.

Integration Specialist: The *Integration Specialist* is responsible for the technical design of any integration needs. Also, the Integration Specialist advises on the selection of an integration tool and the design of the integration process. This role can both deliver and govern the execution of integration deliverables.

Data Architect: The *Data Architect* is responsible for performing data migrations by developing a mapping document for importing data. The Data Architect advises on a strategy for the data migration process and executes the data load.

Success Manager: The *Success Manager* is responsible for working with your organization after implementation is complete to support ongoing maintenance requests. Also, the Support Manager may assist with system administration including coordinating configuration, development, data and integration services. Additional Support Manager services may be defined in the Support Statement of Work, if applicable.

The Client Roles

In addition to development specific resources you may have business resources.

Product Owner: This is a single point of contact who will be responsible for both defining and communicating the overall business vision of and requirements for the solution to the broader team. The Product Owner will work collaboratively with the Development team in the initial development and prioritization of the backlog and ongoing backlog management, including refinement and prioritization of user stories. The Product Owner will be responsible for engaging subject matter experts, facilitating internal decision making and communicating decisions back to the Development team. The Product Owner's attendance to relevant meetings is required for the successful delivery of the project. The best Product Owner may not be a technical resource, but rather, a person who knows the business well and will be able to provide the direction required to fully realize business value of the initiative. Participation by the Product Owner on a daily basis throughout the project is vital to its success.

Project Team: During the ramp period of your project, you should assemble a project team that includes representatives from the various groups that will be included under this initiative (e.g., sales, marketing, service delivery management, engagement management, etc.) The role of this team will be to ensure the detailed requirements of the users are represented in the user stories. This team will participate in solution demos at the completion of each sprint to provide feedback on the solution progress. We recommend this project team be maintained beyond the completion of the initiative and serve as a group that can review enhancement requests as well as measure the success of the project against its original objectives.

System Administrator: This position may or may not be the same as the Product Owner. This individual will be responsible for ongoing maintenance of the final systems that are implemented, e.g. CRM,

Marketing Automation, Case Management platform etc.

Post Implementation Resources

These can be internal employees, contractors or freelancers. Sometimes its agency resources that provide team members or done for you services.

Marketing

Growth Hacker: Marketers, engineers and product managers that specifically focus on building and engaging the user base of a business

Digital Marketing Manager: Responsible for creating and managing digital marketing campaigns. Use a range of techniques including paid search, SEO and PPC, email marketing. Might also oversee the social media strategy for the company. Responsible for managing online brand and product campaigns to raise brand awareness

Sales

Sales Development Representatives (SDR): is a type of inside sales rep that focuses on outbound prospecting. Many companies (such as Salesforce) have experienced massive revenue growth by separating **sales** organizations into specific roles.

Business Development Representatives (BDR): While a sales representative or Account Executive works with existing clients to keep them happy and serve their needs, business development reps seek out and build new business for their enterprise.

251

Account Executives (Managers, Sales Representatives): Depending upon your business size and the size and complexity of customers, these are the closers and they manage active Sales Opportunities.

Partner/Channel Managers: The Channel Partner Manager or Partner Manager is responsible for selling products and services to customers primarily through third-party relationships like resellers, affiliate, VAR or integration Partners.

Customer Service/Support/Success

Customer Service Manager: These team members make sure that the needs of their customers are being satisfied. Their aim is to provide excellent customer service answer questions, resolving product, service or account-related problems through various channels of support, e.g. telephone, email, social media.

Customer Success Manager: more proactive than Customer Service Managers, this role is about outreach to existing clients. Particularly in SaaS software businesses or those with ongoing service agreements or revenue models, this relationship focused role is all about retention and optimization.

Where to Find Team Resources

Here are some of my favorite online locations to source either full-time or part-time freelancer team members.

   a. Upwork.com
   b. Fiverr.com
   c. LinkedIn.com
   d. Craigslist.com

e. University Co-Op or Placement: check out your local community college or University they always have a department for outplacement of grads or summer student. (Well, usually.)

f. http://www.simplyhired.com/

g. https://www.indeed.com

h. http://www.internships.com/

i. Startup Events: There are lots of these but check out WeWork.com or other co-working spaces

j. meetup.com for startup events or groups specific to the role you're looking to hire for. There are meetups for marketing, sales, customer support, specific software applications, growth hacking and the list goes on.

k. Referrals and Recommendations: ask for referrals from colleagues on Facebook, LinkedIn, even Twitter

l. Throw a Party or a recruiting event.

Chapter Summary Points

1. Building both a short-term and long-term project team will involve many stakeholders.

2. Long-term success will still depend on having key roles in Marketing, Sales, and Customer Support.

3. There will also have to be technology and product experts along with business leadership roles to consider, some of which like Growth Hackers, Sales Development Representative or Customer Success Managers that are non-traditional.

Chapter 9: Taking action on your Automate and Grow plan

Presumably, now you've been through the entire book.

With your own Automate and Grow Strategic Plan and the right team you are armed to transform your business.

This is where the fun begins.

Creating a Strategy was the first step into a bigger world. The second step however involves the actual implementation of new software, systems, digital products and services.

Creating these can be challenging. The fruits of this are going to be at the end of actual software implementation, development, customization and training.

Be forewarned, the path forward will potentially have challenging moments.

In part any digital transformation should be approached in stages. Record incremental wins.

There are four things you should have in place going forward though that will potentially change the trajectory of your business

   - Clear business positioning
   - Foundation to create your own Monopoly Business as defined by Peter Thiel

- Automated systems to address Marketing, Sales and Customer Support
- Digital Innovation by the application of SaaS, mobile apps and digital processes and systems to improve both Operational Excellence and enhance the Customer Journey

Your Traffic and Conversion Plan defines your target audiences, and how you will use both marketing automation, web sites, apps and social channels to target, attract and convert your ideal customers into prospects for your business. This is a key driver of your growth as you build up new leads, prospects, and opportunities on a scalable basis.

Then, we also created your Sales Playbook. This defines how you take prospects and guide them through their Sales Journey. Using our sales process and funnel, we employ both technology and people to close sales opportunities and transactions with new and existing clients.

This might be using e-commerce and other tools to complete digital transactions or a sales team, possibly inbound or outbound to help customers either through a complex product, service or software sale. Or a complex organization that needs much information and help to make purchasing decisions.

This is where you want to use CRM technology to scale sales funnels and so your implementation plan will be to both train, manage and execute sales strategy as well as supporting technologies like apps, SaaS, CRM, websites, and other digital tools for sales automation

Finally, your Customer Success Roadmap defines your Customer Experience. Once you've acquired a customer and they've made a purchase with you, how you proactively work to keep them as a customer. In the case where you have software as a service other recurring revenue services, this approach retains revenue and will be critical to growth.

This is how you keep customers happily invested in your business. This will also define how you use case management technology, websites, a knowledge base, customer communities, apps and other tools to deliver a more consistent customer success experience across all customers you acquire.

Finally an implementation plan you created to define the technology, people and tactical resources you will use to achieve your new business objectives.

This implementation plan will give your Automate and Grow team the framework they need to implement new platforms for marketing automation, Customer Relationship Management software and case management software. As well as all of the customizations and automations within each of these applications.

I hope that this invigorates you. It is an exciting process that you and your business have decided to follow. Take this as an opportunity to create a culture in your business that is focused upon automating important and repetitive tasks, while empowering people to innovate. I hope this empowers you to strive for customer delight and to work towards a more dynamic and exciting organization.

_____

> Without continual growth and progress, such words as improvement, achievement, and success have no meaning.

- Benjamin Franklin

———————

Take the 30 Day Challenge: 30 Days to An Automate and Grow Strategic Plan
http://www.automategrow.biz/30daychallenge

Your Notes

What are your big three takeaways from Automate and Grow? Write them down here:

1._____
_____
_____

2._____
_____
_____

3._____
_____
_____

What are your first three steps to creating an Automate and Grow Strategy, plan and culture? Write them down here:

1._____
_____

2._____
_____

3._____
_____